"At a time when conscious journaling is trending, *Dream Du'a Do* is a must-have resource for the modern Muslim woman. With a tone that's engaging and relatable, combining nods to pop culture with deeper religious ideals, the book will appeal to young Muslimahs across the globe. Traditional 'Islamic' guides and self-help books are often dry and impersonal, but *Dream Du'a Do* is balanced and interactive, reflecting on the inspiring stories of female Muslim role models while encouraging self-reflection from a refreshing framework of faith."

Hafsa Lodi, journalist and author of *Modesty: A Fashion Paradox*

"Ruzina writes with such optimism and depth it makes you know that the dreams you have are worth the chase. The one thing that this book makes clear is that it's our willingness to dream and have faith through our du'as that ultimately give us the strength to do what it takes to fulfil our dreams."

Rabina Khan, journalist and author of *My Hair is Pink Under This Veil*

dream
du'a
do

A Millennial Muslimah's Guide
to Achieving Your Wildest Dreams

Ruzina Ahad

THE
DREAMWORK
COLLECTIVE

This edition was published by The Dreamwork Collective
The Dreamwork Collective LLC, Dubai, United Arab Emirates
thedreamworkcollective.com

Printed and bound in the United Arab Emirates by Al Ghurair Printing & Publishing

Cover, design and inside illustrations: Kasia Piątek, kasiapiatek.pl

Text © Ruzina Ahad, 2021

ISBN 978-9948-8719-3-4

Approved by National Media Council Dubai, United Arab Emirates
MC-02-01-0159795

The content of this book is appropriate for all age groups according to the age
classification system issued by the Ministry of Culture and Youth.

For my Moshi Monsters,
Never stop dreaming.

Contents

Introduction

As-salaamu alaikum! Well hello, you!

I'm guessing that if I were to ask how you were doing, you'd tell me that in the grand scheme of things, you're doing pretty okay? You've got a roof over your head, you've got a family you can cope with *most* of the time, but most importantly, you've got Wi-Fi, which means you get to post those lovely pictures of your outfit of the day or the bougie eggs Benedict you ate for brunch.

But just like the younger, more foolish version of me, perhaps sometimes you feel that even though you seemingly *do* have everything, something still seems to be missing. Some days you're grateful for what you have, but other days you feel like a sad karaoke version of a Britney Spears song gone wrong on loop.

You can't quite point your finger to what it is, but something is definitely missing; you feel it in the core of your being and in the way you go about your Barry average day, and when you stand in front of the mirror, all you see is your outraged reflection pointing a finger back at you, yelling... "Ya basic!"

Sis, I feel your pain! I've been there. I've heard those tiny high-pitched voices in my head telling me that so much more is out there waiting for me, but I've also heard louder voices telling me that I don't deserve it and that I'm going to fail. "Dreams are for dreamers," they say. "Real people have to work hard, have mouths to feed, and have taxes to pay."

And yet dreams are sold to us daily, aren't they? They're plastered all over our Pinterest boards, they're photoshopped on the covers of our magazines, heard in the songs that are played when we're grocery shopping, and scattered over our social media feeds.

As I reflect on the time when I didn't know what my big dream was, I remember feeling as though I was always stuck with a choice to make: Either I had to choose between dreams for my *dunya* (my world), or dreams for my *deen* (my religion). I never thought I could choose both.

I've always been a bit of a bookworm, so naturally I sought wisdom by burying my head in a pile of self-improvement books. But the problem with most of the books I read was that they were asking me to trust the universe instead of trusting God, the Maker, which never quite sat right with me.

In Islam, the term used for self-improvement is *tazkiyah*, and even though striving to become the best version of ourselves is fundamentally what our faith is about, living as a Muslim in a non-Muslim country, I struggled to understand *tazkiyah* and as a result wasted many years struggling to become the greatest version of me.

Although I stumbled onto some amazing literary masterpieces on how to go about being successful in this life, very rarely did I come across easy-to-read, modern books that would also show me how to prepare for success in the afterlife.

When I searched for bestsellers on *a Muslim's guide to dreaming big*, guess what? I found none. There are over a billion Muslims dotted around the world; surely I couldn't be the only whacko with a burning desire to read something like that?

Over time, I discovered oodles of useful prayers to recite, a plethora of translated advice from myriad renowned Arabic scholars, but none that would speak to me directly in my language—in plain and simple English. And so I decided to write a book that would do just that.

Now, I don't know if I have it all figured out, but what I do know is that through trial and tears, I've figured out enough to live a life that I love. So, if not for anyone else, these words are a letter to my younger self, for that insecure little girl who became a woman based on an identity entirely narrated by the aftermath of 9/11 and the War on Terror.

This book is about everything I learned on the journey I took to get here, to reach a point where I can share knowledge that will prevent you making the same mistakes I did when it came to chasing my wildest dreams.

This book is a trumpet call to you, to push past everything you know to be true and manifest the life you've always dreamed of. A call that I wish I'd heard during those difficult teenage years when I often questioned myself as to who I was becoming and what I *really* wanted for my future.

Think of this reading experience as a conversation about self-discovery. It is a book about you developing the tools you need so you can become the best version of yourself, so you can go out there and achieve your most audacious ambitions.

I think you'll value the fact that this is a seriously simple book. You'll be pleased to find that it's not filled with overcomplicated jargon, lengthy discussions of verses from the Quran, or even longer narrations of the chains of narrations of a particular *hadith*.

Instead, what you will find are thoughts and theories based on Islamic theology, neuroscience, and positive psychology. Along the way, I share cool tips and techniques that helped change my mindset and eventually helped change my life. I'm hoping they'll change yours too.

Don't worry, I'm not about to share yet another weird and wonderful story about how I built a million-dollar tech company from scratch, or how I became a celebrity overnight through a video that went viral on the internet, and I most definitely won't be sharing before and after pictures of my dramatic weight loss journey to show how you too can become a hotcake just like me.

Instead, what I do share is tactical advice for how to go about achieving your craziest dreams. I've done all the reading and researching so you don't have to. So, sit back and enjoy a hot cup of cocoa whilst I indulge you with everything I've learned so far.

How to Use this Book

By the time you've reached the end of this book, I want you to be a living example of a transformational philosophy that I've lived by for the best part of a decade. I firmly believe that to be, to have, or to conquer virtually anything you want, you need to be able to do three things: Dream, Du'a, and Do.

This book, therefore, is split into three glorious parts. The first part focuses on dreaming. We will take a whistle-stop tour on why it's so important to dream, what we've been getting wrong about dreaming, and why so many of us are held back from dreaming big.

The second part of the book focuses on a revolutionary act of worship that we all know as du'a. Loosely translated, du'a is an Arabic term used to describe the act of making a prayer. In this section we will look at the art of making du'a and discuss why it is so crucial to living a life that you love.

The third part of the book focuses on action. I walk you through seven non-negotiable actions that I took to be able to achieve multiple

> **My deepest du'a is that my words help you navigate closer toward becoming the Muslimah you need to become in order to do what you were divinely designed to do.**

dreams, and as I do so I hope you learn why it's so important to be laser-focused and single-minded about the pursuit of achieving your own wildest dreams.

By the time you've read the last page of this book, I want you to have a very clear vision of your life and know exactly what you want, why you want it, and what you're going to do next in order to achieve it.

My recommendation is to take the time to answer as many of the questions and prompts as you can. There are plenty of spaces to fill with your scribbles, doodles, questions, and thoughts. Go all out circling and underlining the bits that resonate with you so you can go back to them later. Get a highlighter ready to skim and scan for Pinterest-worthy quotes, dog-ear your favourite pages, do whatever you want to make this book your own.

If you don't speak Arabic, you'll be glad to know that any Arabic words mentioned in this book are written in a transliterated form in English. I explain most of the meanings as I go and there's also a glossary for you to refer to. You'll also notice that I've avoided writing the verses of the Quran and *hadith* in Arabic and instead used the translated verses, for a smoother reading experience.

Finally, as you know, it is customary to glorify Allah (*Subhanahu Wa Ta'ala*) and to send salutations upon Prophet Muhammad (*sallalahu Alaihi Wassalam*) as well as to send peace and blessings on all our prophets, their families and companions each time their names are mentioned. For a smoother read, I assume that you know the drill, and I'll leave it to you to glorify God and send salutations as and when needed.

I sincerely hope that you enjoy reading the book as much as I enjoyed writing it. The tips and techniques I've acquired have changed my life, and I can't wait to find out that they have inspired you to change yours too.

Creating a remarkable life is absolutely within our reach, especially for those of us who dare to **Dream**, rely on the power of **Du'a**, and then go out to **Do** whatever it takes to achieve our wildest, most outrageous goals. Your mission now, should you choose to accept it, is to join me on this incredible journey to Dream, make Du'a, then Do.

Are you ready?

STEP 1:

dream

CHAPTER ONE

Finding the One

Welcome aboard on the greatest adventure—your life—and may I say how honoured I feel to be tagging along with you!

Consider this first part of your journey as the planning stage. I'm hoping that you'll laugh a little and learn a lot as we take a whistle-stop tour on what it means to dream big and wake up to your most awesome ambitions. Along the way, you'll also get to meet some marvellous Muslimahs just like you who will inspire you to think about why dreaming big is interconnected with our faith.

I can't promise that what lies ahead will be a smooth ride, but I can promise that by the end of this chapter you'll have the answer to the most important question you've probably asked all day. No, not 'Siri, what's the weather like?' But...

What is your big dream?

We hear and see it all the time, don't we? Dream house, dream spouse, dream wedding, dream job, dream holiday, dream car... the list goes on and on, whirling around us at a dizzying speed.

Call it what you like, a wish, an ambition, or a burning desire to accomplish a vision. However you want to word it, I believe that dreams are what make your life worth living. They are the reason why you wake up in the morning and why you persevere through to the night. Had my heart been deprived of my weird and wonderful dreams, I just know that I wouldn't be living the life I love today.

Dreams are wishful thinking, if you will; they are those little voices in your head that randomly pop up as you go about your business. You could be praying *salah*, or making an omelette, or at the spa getting a pedicure, and up they pop, in all shapes and sizes.

Throughout human history, we have used the great 'imagine if' sentence to achieve spectacular outcomes. And that's how all great accomplishments start, don't they? With a simple prompt about imagining that a certain possibility, if pursued, could turn into something quite remarkable.

Those sporadic bursts of 'imagine ifs' are very much needed in our lives because without them, we would be lost, wandering around with no real sense of purpose, always on the lookout but never really knowing what it is we're looking for. Dreaming big is a necessary part of being a Muslimah because without our dreams, we would feel hopeless, waking up with no real plans to pursue apart from eating, sleeping, and fiddling with our filters for that perfect selfie.

That 'imagine if'? Listen carefully to it because it is your future to-do list, to-be list, or even to-learn list. It didn't make it to the forefront of your attention by accident; it had to combat its way through a gazillion other things, all fighting for your kind consideration. It is there for a divine purpose. It is tugging at you to tell you where to go next, if only you would just wake up and pay attention.

It was at university that I first became curious about not only my dreams but also what others dreamed of. My favourite (but slightly creepy) hobby was making up wild stories about the tired-looking strangers sitting opposite me on the train. Most of the stories were so elaborate that I would burst into random fits of giggles, but sometimes, I would look at their frazzled faces and wonder at which point they decided to get "real" and stop dreaming.

Where along the way did they lose sight of the infinite possibilities? When did they decide to settle for an ordinary life?

I would also look around my own community and wonder how the same faith could propel some people to live such rich, interesting, and inspired lives while others remained unmoved, submitting to being passive passengers on the greatest train journey of their life. How could this be possible when we all read the same words from the same Quran? Pretty deep for a commute home at 4.30 p.m., I know.

I have always been a bit of a daydreamer; I was forever getting in trouble at home and at school for having my head in the clouds. As a child, I would grab a hairbrush and pretend to be a singer one day, whereas on other days I would have a clipboard and pen in hand, pretending to be a high-flying news reporter. As a child I truly believed that I could become one of those things (and just in case 0.2 percent of you are wondering, I am tone deaf, so no! I didn't end up getting four big yeses from Simon Cowell and his fellow judges on *The X Factor...*)

Looking around me, I struggled to understand why so many others seemed to have lost sight of their big dreams.

Now, I don't have any scientific research to back this up (yet), but I suspect the answer to my question is that by the time we become fully fledged adults, some of us lose touch with our big dreams—or never even discover what our big dreams were—because we were far too busy fulfilling the dreams that other people had for us.

I highly doubt that any of us have said, 'Inshallah! I can't wait to grow up and get my nose squashed up against the train door during rush hour every day to work for someone else's dreams instead of my own!' And yet here we are, doing just that, living a life that we know, deep down, is far removed from living a life we love.

As we muddled our way through growing up, growing careers, or growing families, many of us convinced ourselves that we just weren't good enough to pursue whatever it was we wanted for our future selves. And even if we pondered for a fleeting moment that Allah had a purpose for us, that thought was quickly derailed by proper priorities, such as miniature mouths to feed, mortgages to maintain, and monthly Netflix subscriptions to pay.

It's as if we simply woke up one morning and decided that our ambitions were far too outrageous, too unrealistic, and too irrational to ever be accomplished.

By the time I grew up into a miserable teen, I'd forgotten the big dreams I dreamt up as a little girl. As I sat on the train, watching other people and letting my own life chug on by, I became good at suppressing those inner voices that asked questions I couldn't answer. I focused on my mundane routine and walked on the safer side of the road, because finding my feet and figuring out my purpose drained me.

I began to lose my zest for dreaming big until one day I finally realised what my big dream was truly supposed to be.

My epiphany came whilst reciting *Surah al Ankabut* (29:64), where we are clearly told what our big dream should be. Allah tells us that:

"this worldly life is no more than play and amusement. But the hereafter is indeed the real life, if only they knew".

See, my big dream, your big dream, and quite frankly all our big dreams should be one thing and one thing only: to ultimately enter Paradise. Everything else is our side hustle. When we dream, we should dream the crème de la dream, which is to enter our home in

the hereafter, the place where our wonderful Messenger describes
that there would be bounties

> **"no eye (has ever) seen,
> no ear has (ever) heard and
> no human heart has ever perceived."
> (Muslim:2824b)**

And so, as I read those precious words in the Holy Quran, I realised
that if I believe there is no deity worth worshipping but Allah and that
Muhammad is the final Messenger, there is a very real possibility of
entering either Heaven or Hell. If I believe our souls will live on and
on for eternity, I need to dream a dream that transcends this lifetime
and ensures that I live happily ever after, forever.

Going to *Jannah* is the big dream.

Individually, we may have lots of other dreams, but collectively, our
only purpose is to live a life pleasing to Al Khaliq, our Creator, so we
can be rewarded with eternity in Paradise.

This truth isn't reserved exclusively for Muslims; it's for anyone who believes in a higher power, in God, in Judgement Day, and in the final destinations we universally know as Heaven or Hell.

We have been chasing this dream since the beginning of human history, and we have been reminded to achieve this divine dream over and over again through all God's guidebooks—the Torah, the Gospel, the Psalms, and the scrolls—but for one reason or another, along the way some of us just forgot.

Perhaps the idea of Heaven is far too complicated to imagine, which is why many of us drown ourselves with distractions that we mistake for our dreams. We fill our lives with other ambitions, such as relationship goals, retirement goals, or Harry Potter–loving, skinny jeans–wearing, make sure you take plenty of pics or you didn't *really* go travelling goals, but they never fulfil us because we are so disconnected from our God-given dream.

Some of us recognise that attaining Paradise is our one true purpose, but we get lazy and don't work for it. We lock it away on the "things to review when I'm just about to die" side of our brain, and in doing so, we lose focus on our actual purpose in life. We take our big dream of entering *Jannah* for granted because we foolishly assume that just because we are believers, we are somehow all guaranteed Heaven. Hell, no!

Our darling Prophet compared the temporariness of the *dunya* to taking a break under a shade tree: After we've rested, we get up, leave, and continue our journey. Any dream or ambition that you harbour in your heart, therefore, is a sub-dream, a stepping-stone, a *dunya* dream. They are a means to use so we can continue toward our destination: the magnificent gates of Paradise.

If you genuinely want to live a life that you love, you need to allow this big dream of entering Paradise to permeate into your smaller dreams. It must become a way of life rather than just something you were told to believe. In the next chapter we will explore how to connect your *deen* to your *dunya* dream, but for now you need to unequivocally accept the fact that first and foremost, to Allah we belong and to Allah we will return, and that needs to shine through everything you do.

At this point, some of you may be feeling despair, thinking, Aaahhh! What if I'm just trying to get through the working week as pain free as possible and fit in as many laughing emojis and lols as I can at the end of my WhatsApp messages? What if I don't have a *dunya* dream?

Panic not, sweet friend! Of course you do! You just haven't discovered it yet.

YET. Those three precious letters you've just read without giving them a second thought, don't underestimate them because that word is atomic! The way I see it, *yet* is an emblem for promises and possibilities. *Yet* symbolises what is to come and the reason we must keep pushing forward.

See, every single one of us is born with a special gift from Allah, known as talent. Talent is what I would describe as *noor*, a tiny beam of light that shines brightly within the hearts of some and dimly resides in the hearts of others. But regardless, it is there inside each of us, lighting us up in our own unique ways.

Some people spend their entire lives searching for their light, so don't lose hope if you haven't discovered what your *dunya* dream is, yet. I'm positive that you'll find the answer the minute you start looking. It will appear everywhere you turn, whispering in your ear, tugging at your heart, and consuming your head until you find your light.

Your Turn!

Allah has already told us what our big dream is, so you can use this section to reaffirm it. But what I really want you to focus on in this section are your smaller dreams, your *dunya* dreams. They can come in all shapes and sizes and can be anything that you wish for. And they can be used as a starting point.

Here are a few things you may find useful when thinking about your *dunya* dreams:

→ Not all dreams need to be worthy of the Nobel Peace Prize. Think of a couple of crazy dreams, then choose your favourite.
→ What are some of your regrets?
→ What are some of the things you wish you could have accomplished if you had the time and money?
→ Explore dreams for different areas of your life, e.g., spiritual/social/ financial/relational/educational/physical.

Jot down your ideas here
Explore dreams for different areas of your life:

relationships

spirituality

My
big dream

My *dunya* dreams

Meet Fatima Al Fihri

A Fabulous Founder

Fatima Al Fihri was Tunisian and founded the world's first university.

Did you know...

- Fatima was born in the ninth century and was renowned for her extensive knowledge of Islam and architecture. She combined her talents and opened the doors to the world's first—and now the world's oldest—university.
- The Al Qarrawiyyin masjid and university can still be found in Fez, Morocco, and is regarded as the oldest academic institute in the world.
- Fatima's father was a wealthy businessman who left her a huge inheritance when he died, but instead of wasting it, she used her resources to invest not just in herself but also in the generations to come after her.

"Because of me,
there are universities."

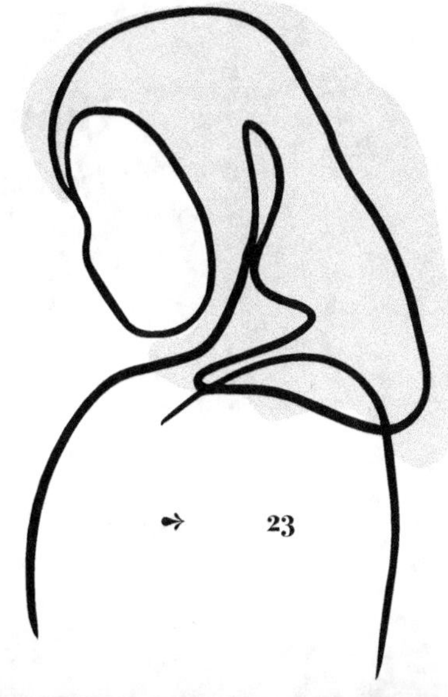

CHAPTER TWO

Connecting the Dots

Your purpose was divinely assigned the moment you were created, but finding that purpose is a voyage in itself. It will require some real soul searching and a little head scratching. In this chapter, you'll need to fasten your spiritual seatbelt as we discuss how to connect your big holy dream (*deen*) to your smaller dreams (*dunya*).

Think of this chapter as a holy version of Tripadvisor where we'll be exploring a variety of places to visit before you reach your final destination. You may experience some motion sickness as you try to bridge your dreams between the here and now and the hereafter, but don't worry, I promise to be with you all the way as we answer:

How can your *dunya* dream be connected to your *deen*?

Making the connection between your *dunya* dream and your *deen* isn't always easy. You may find that what you want for yourself in this life is completely unrelated to the next life.

For example, if your dream is to own a shiny red Ferrari, how will that help you get on the highway to Heaven? Or if your dream is to knock down a wall to renovate your existing house into your dream house, you might be wondering, how that will help you knock on Heaven's door?

When I struggled to find a good *dunya* dream, the question I had to ask myself was, What do I have to do to put my bum on a first-class seat to *Jannah*?

To answer that question, you need to think about what you have been placed on Earth to achieve. Is it through being woke and fighting for social justice? Is it through healing? Through informing, educating, or entertaining? What are your special gifts?

There are so many ways to explore how best you can make your dream of entering Paradise a reality, so I reckon now would be a good time to take yourself out on a date, order a latte with double shots of caramel, take out your notebook, and try to figure out what you want to do with the rest of your life.

Here's a little secret I discovered too late into my twenties: Knowing what you want often reveals itself when you start focusing on how to use your potential to serve others instead of worrying how it will serve you.

Luckily for us, Allah has told us what our purpose is, but then with that purpose, you need to identify how your dream will help you do the following two things:

1. Love Allah
2. Love others

How you show your love can be manifested in so many ways. You may want to begin with taking a look at some of the wonderful Muslimahs mentioned throughout this book, or at other people you consider as role models. Think about how they have connected their *dunya* dream to the *akhira* by serving Allah as well as serving others.

Dreams come in all shapes and sizes and there is no one way to love Allah and love others.

Your dream may be to defy the odds and shatter glass ceilings, to pave the way for others. Or your idea of being of service may be in inspiring, leading a revolution, and making your mark in the world despite what society tells you. Or it may be the case of travelling with purpose, to go hajj or to build hospitals or schools or rebuild homes in war-torn countries. Or being of service could mean quietly creating art, growing a garden, or writing poems.

All you need to do is figure out what lights you up.

Now, you may be thinking that this is a total waste of your time because in a world where we are spoilt with so many options, even if you did come up with a goal, how on earth are you meant to know that you've found your true calling?

Here's my two pennies worth: If my own dreams are anything to go by, I can tell you that when you do eventually stumble across *it*, every part of you will have this bizarre sense of happiness and harmony all at once. This sense of, I can't quite put it into words, but it just *feels* right.

In the words of Marie Kondo, it will simply "spark joy".

It will creep up in your quietest prayers; it will be stirring conversations while hanging out with your friends in fancy cafes, or smoking shisha late at night. When you finally meet your destiny, you will feel a sense of divine responsibility, that for reasons unknown, somehow this job is meant to be done by only you.

How you connect your everyday dreams, your lofty dreams, and all the other in-between dreams to pleasing God depends on your answers to a handful of questions. At first sight they might appear pretty simple, but once you begin to dig deeper, you'll discover that they are actually some of the most complicated questions you can ask yourself.

1.   Who are you?
2.   Where are you?
3.   What do you want?
4.   Why do you want it?
5.   How are you going to achieve it?

I discovered that nearly all the personal development literature I devoured over the last decade attempted to answer these same questions in one form or another.

As we work our way through this book I'll help you find answers to these questions, but you may also find it useful to scribble down some thoughts too.

My hope is that as you go about organising your thoughts around the answers to these life-defining questions, you'll start connecting your goals to the unique purpose Allah created you for, both in this world and the next.

Who are you?

Figuring out who you are plays a vital role in discovering where your future dreams lie. When I ask *Who are you?* I'm not asking about your name, your gender, or your ethnicity. I'm asking you to dig deeper to understand who you *really* are. I'm asking you to think about who you are representing today in this modern world.

We *are* Muslimahs, you guys!

We are the flag bearers of our *ummah* today, and though we may stagger, we may trip, and we may fall flat on our faces along the way, *we* are the ones who will pass the baton forward to the future *ummah* tomorrow!

Know that we were not created by accident; we were created to butterfly. We were created to grow and change and to better not just ourselves but also everyone around us, to create a ripple effect of fiercely inspirational women just like our predecessors and our predecessors before that.

This is *who* we are. Millennial Muslimahs. Women of unparalleled power.

The world needs who you are, who you were meant to be. When you give yourself permission to dream big and allow yourself to unleash the potential within you, not only will you change your life, but you will change all of ours as well.

Where are you?

And before you ask, nope! I'm not asking about where you are geographically, nor am I asking where you are emotionally or spiritually. Though if your faith has hit an all-time low, you're lost in the Amazonian rainforest, or you're stuck in a dead-end job or an unhealthy marriage, I'd definitely encourage you to have a conversation with yourself. But what I am asking you to ask yourself is *Where do you think you stand* in the world today?

Let's look at some facts. Over a third of today's Muslims are under thirty. This means that while the Western population is aging, the Muslim population is young and growing. The future is ours to own, if we want it.

Somewhere, inside us all, lives the potential to change the world.

Here's another fact. By the year 2030, Muslims are expected to populate at least a third of the world. This means that with more than 50 percent of the Muslim population under thirty, our spending power is what the global fashion, food, travel, cosmetics, and care industries are scrambling to attract because we are worth billions. With the rise of Muslim influencers in practically every industry, can you imagine what our worth will be in another decade's time?

We live in an era where our attention is valuable. Our spending power is significant, and our opinions are not only important but highly sought after. We matter. For the first time in our lifetime, we're witnessing a phenomenal shift in the negative narrative we grew up hearing.

Twenty years ago, we couldn't even dream of seeing women like us, women who are visibly Muslim, dressed in hijab, representing us in politics, in media, or even in sports. But over the last ten years we've started seeing a rise of strong Muslim women everywhere.

This is where we are. This is where you are.

You are in a place where you hold a very powerful key to the future, and that future needs you, your voice and your vision, now more than ever. You are exactly where your Maker wants you to be. You are the revolution.

So, when trying to connect the dots, ask yourself what you want to do with this privilege, this passion, this power, this incredible opportunity we, as Muslim women, have been given today.

There are so many industries painfully lacking representation from us, just waiting to see Muslimahs like us shatter glass ceilings to create new history.

Just in case we never meet and I never get to say this to your face, I want you to know that your opinion matters, your ideas matter. *You matter.* So, what extraordinary gift will you share with the world?

Lady, you are standing at the pinnacle of a revolution about to happen.

What do you want?

This is probably the toughest question you can ask yourself. A good place to start is to think about what you are curious about or what you are passionate about.

Not knowing what you want to do, be, or have right now isn't a problem—it's a fun puzzle. Take your time! But before you get obsessed with the pursuit of finding just one big thing to do with the rest of your life, here's a thought inspired by Morpheus from *The Matrix*: *What if I told you* that our time here in this world doesn't have to begin and end with just one big calling? *What if I told you* that we can carry many little dreams that grow and change with us as we age?

As I learned more about my faith and realised that my purpose was to worship Allah so that I can enter *Jannah*, I realised that everything I do, including the pursuit of my dreams, is a declaration of worshipping Allah. You too have been gifted with a with a bunch of callings that will help you earn extra *Jannah* points and become the person God intended you to be.

All you have to do is figure out what you're designed to do.

Your Turn!

Use this space to think about connecting the dots between your *dunya* and your *deen.*

Remember that no one is judging you here. This is for your eyes only, so keep it authentic. Don't scribble down something worthy or extra holy if that's not actually what you really want and in line with your talents and passions.

Go ahead and have that much-needed conversation with yourself. Ask yourself what gift you have been given. What creative potential do you have in you that will speak for you long after you're gone? What is that one big thing you need to do to get you one step closer to achieving the ultimate dream? What gesture of love for Allah are you going to share with the world?

In this season of my life, my *dunya* dream is to share my message with you, and the way I connect it to my *deen* is by writing a book that I hope will inspire Muslims everywhere, and to impart knowledge, which is an act of *sadaqah Jariyah.*

What are my gifts?

How can I connect my *dunya* dream to my *deen*?

  ← dream

Meet Ibtihaj Mohammad

An Amazing Athlete

Ibtihaj is an American sabre fencer who was the first American woman to compete in the Olympics in a hijab.

Did you know...

→ Ibtihaj was not only the first American to compete at the Olympics in a hijab but also the first Muslim American woman to win a medal.

→ Ibtihaj is an activist shattering stereotypes for Muslim women. She is a fashion designer and launched a modest fashion label, Louella, as well as helping Nike develop the Pro Hijab.

"We are all born with something that God has given us and we owe it to ourselves to discover what that gift is, and to change our families, our communities, and the world. I truly believe our purpose is to leave a positive mark on the world."

CHAPTER THREE

The F Word

In this chapter we'll take a look at some of the stumbling blocks we may face when we try to accomplish our goals. There will also be lots of groundwork for you to do, and you'll need to venture to a few places you've never been as we take a slight detour to explore some things that can prevent you achieving your wildest dreams.

There's a lot to unpack here, so you might want to bring a toothbrush and a sleeping bag in case you need to camp overnight. If you happen to own a torch (the flashlight on your phone will do) you may want to bring that too, as we dive deep underground and shine a light on

What is holding you back from dreaming big?

I bet you're wondering that if all it takes to live a life you love is to simply dream big, why isn't everyone dreaming big? The answer to that is simple: The world around us makes us feel so small that it prevents us dreaming big. I know this all too well because once upon a time, I lived there too.

The biggest reason I struggled to achieve what I truly wanted is because I lived in a space where my dreams were limited, not just internally but also externally. Looking back, it totally makes sense why I struggled with achieving any of my lofty goals because for so long I lived in an environment where everywhere I turned, I was met with frazzled faces or blank stares.

I lived in a world where negativity encircled me. I mixed with people who were only truly happy when they were complaining. It took a certain level of discomfort to unearth this, but the reality for me was that I was a product of the thinking around me. And so, for the longest time, much of my dreaming was small.

I was born and bred in the East End of London, a place where, regardless of our differences in who we worshipped or how much we earned, complaining incessantly as we sipped our way through cups of tea was our favourite pastime. It was the only sensible way we knew how to keep calm and carry on.

I mean, can we even call ourselves proud Eastenders if we can't enjoy a good old rant about the weather, the neighbours, the NHS, the government, the taxes, the traffic, Brexit, Mexit, the fact that it's Monday, and basically anything and everything?

Another reason I couldn't dream as big as I wanted to was because I grew up in an era when I was constantly led to believe that the world didn't have space for girls who looked like me. It didn't take long for me to look around and realise that even if I felt my dreams were limitless, the opportunity to fulfil any of those dreams was limited.

I was schooled that way. I went through my entire formal education not once being taught by a teacher wearing hijab. Years later, when

I entered the working world as an educator myself, I was literally the only visibly Muslim woman around.

When I watched TV as a child, the closest I got to seeing a hijab on TV was Whoopie Goldberg dressed as a nun in *Sister Act*. I wanted to watch superhero movies where the protagonist would come flying down in a cape and a hijab (I still do). I wanted to play with Barbie dolls that were dressed like me and read books with characters that looked like me.

As I grew more aware of my faith during my teens, I wanted to read Islamic books and listen to inspirational lectures *by* women *for* women just like me. When I went to the masjid to sit at *halaqas* (study circles), I wanted to be told how to behave like an *ideal Muslimah* not by a man but by a woman, just like me.

They say you can't be what you don't see, and what I never saw was me. It seemed that whether I flicked through the pages of my teen magazine or an Islamic book, the messages were all the same: Good Muslim girls were supposed to be seen and not heard.

Never at the forefront, always in the background, quietly co-existing.

We were supposed to be floating around in dowdy dresses, with imaginary wings and halos above our hijabs. We weren't supposed to wave our hands in the air as we unashamedly sang along to pop songs, wave our banners at governments as we protested passionately for human rights, and definitely not supposed to wave two fingers at anyone who tried to confine us.

Everywhere I turned I felt invisible because I lived in a world that had a very clear view of who I should or shouldn't be. And because of that, for the longest time I had limited ambitions.

As a Millennial coming of age in one of the most Islamophobic eras in recent history, combined with the limiting beliefs of the community that surrounded me, it was no wonder dreaming small was so easy.

As I sit here with you and reflect on this, I can't help but feel that the cost of thinking, dreaming, and playing small is by the far the biggest tragedy we're witnessing in modern Muslim history.

For the longest time I couldn't figure out why so many marvellous Muslimahs around me couldn't fight against the standards our environment shackled us with, but I realised that eventually it all boils down to one thing: fear.

Many of us dream small because we're scared. We second-guess ourselves because of the fear of being mocked not only by our nearest and dearest but also by random trolls who themselves are too scared to use their real names when they post their hate on the internet.

Fear is why we underestimate our abilities. Fear is why we seek permission or validation from others and hold back from sharing our God-given talent with the world. Fear is why we hold back from being more assertive and speaking up and as a result almost always end up settling for less than we deserve.

Fear is like a sleeping pit bull terrier that guards the gates of my aspirations. The minute I even try to tiptoe out of my comfort zone and try anything new, I have to brace myself because I'm about to awaken the barking bitch in my head. I'm guessing that you hear her too.

It's the voice that tells you you're not qualified enough, special enough, or strong enough to ever go out there and claim your birthright. It's the voice that rants viciously about the way you look, the way your mouth curls when you speak, or convinces you that no one cares if you want to do anything creative or different with your life.

We hear her in our professional lives where she says we're not smart enough, confident enough, or experienced enough. She rears her ugly head in our personal lives where she tells us we're not competent enough, not just as women but as wives, mothers, daughters, daughters-in-law, or even as friends and co-workers.

The voice of uncertainty is persistent; it is relentless in its efforts to persuade you to not even think about venturing out. It will go on and on until before you know it, you've already hung your hijab out to dry because she convinced you that you just weren't good enough for whatever it is you were supposed to be good at. Why bother at all?

For years I've wrestled with that voice. Usually, I'd be minding my own business, daydreaming and chasing my big lofty goals, and she'd suddenly creep up on me like an old Adele song: "Alloooo, (#wide eyed emoji) it's me..."

Other days she'd trick me into believing that she was my friend and was only looking out for my best interest. She'd argue that she was being realistic and was simply trying to keep me safe. Here's an example: *Don't move abroad, it won't work out and you might die.* She was the voice of reason.

You may want to watch out for that last one because she's far craftier than I ever gave her credit for. For example, you won't just hear a pathetic, weeny voice that panics the minute you take on a new venture, and she definitely won't just plead for you to quit your big audacious goals. Oh no! To completely sabotage your dreams, this voice likes to play games with your mind.

But in all my years of entertaining this chatter in my head, the thing I struggled with most was the two-for-the-price-of-one voice. *Jeeesos! Look at the size of those bingo wings! Didn't you have a baby like ten years ago?!* And as soon as you check yourself out in the mirror and feel mortified by your flabby body, she'll immediately shame your shame: *Sister, there are people literally dying of famine out there and all you can think of is how fat you look? You should be ashamed of yourself!*

Ugh. There is just no winning with this one!

When we leave that voice unchecked, we become so accustomed to listening to it that it almost fades into the background and even becomes a part of us. It doesn't just exist as background noise in the privacy of our minds, it spills over to the way we talk about ourselves to other people and eventually to the way we allow others to talk to us, about us!

I used to spend so much energy finding excuses about why I couldn't be or couldn't do the things I really wanted to do because it was much easier to accept the voice in my head than it was to do the work and see a goal through. At least that way I'd never have to find out that I failed.

But now I can't help but imagine how different the early years of my adulthood would have been if I'd just shut up and showed up for myself? If I just used all my energy to freakin' go for it instead of allowing that nasty voice to talk myself out of it?

Imagine what it would look like for you.

If there's anything I've learned from living with that voice in my head, it's that you won't wake up one day to find that it is suddenly silent. Chances are, you're going to have to silence it. And ten minutes later you're going to have to do it again. And again another ten minutes later, until eventually you'll manage to go a whole ten days or even ten months without being paid a visit.

Here's a quick science lesson for you: There's a part of our brain called the amygdala. This is the part of the brain where the "don't do it" voice lives. The amygdala's main job is to be on high alert for all things scary or dangerous, to protect us. Its other job is to not give a damn whether we're happy or sad.

Obviously, those panic alerts are useful sometimes. For example, you might be tempted to take a dive from a cliff to follow your dream to fly, but fear will creep in and say *Don't do it, girl, don't do it!*, which will then hopefully make you think twice about your actions.

When I understood this simple scientific fact, I began to empathise with the voice in my mad mind and realised that in order to avoid any type of danger, the commander-in-chief of the amygdala hijacks the "aim high" voice as a strategy to stop me experiencing any potential risk of getting my heart broken through failures, disappointments, or criticisms.

It's kind of sweet really.

And so, any time you waste listening to that negative voice, know that it is winning because while you're busy arguing with it and justifying your choices, guess what? That's less time you get to set and crush outrageous goals. Please don't do what I used to do, which is to reason with the voice or reassure it. Instead, what you want to do is raise your hands up as a gesture of surrender and gently sway yourself away from those moaning monologues.

I have found that when I feel overcome with low self-esteem and pessimism, using one of the following strategies to combat my negative self-talk always helps.

"

It breaks my heart
to know that so many
brilliant Muslimahs have given up
on their dreams simply because
they let that vicious voice
drown out the only voice worth
listening to, the voice that
patiently tells them to persevere
and to honour their potential
to do better, to aim high
and be better.

"

1. **Label the voice**

Labelling is powerful because it helps me put into perspective that I am not that voice in my head; that it's not me freaking out but my inner critic.

When I'm having a meltdown, I talk about that voice as if it's someone else. For example, "Oh no! I'm hearing the voice of fear right now". Ask yourself, is the voice you hear the voice of doubt, criticism, anxiety, or something else?

2. **Have some empathy**

When you hear the horrible voice in your head, check in and ask what disappointment, embarrassment, failure, or danger it is trying to save you from.

When you come from a place of compassion, you can acknowledge the voice of fear and failure but also powerfully say thanks but no thanks.

3. **Shake my booty**

Research shows again and again that when you change your physical posture, you change your emotional posture. Anytime I start to feel anxious and like I'm about to freak out, I physically move. Sometimes that could mean simply sitting up straight instead of slouching; other times, depending on how nervous my thoughts make me feel, I get on my treadmill and go for a run, or I put in my ear pods and bop along to a silent disco!

Eventually, it dawned on me that if I didn't stand up for my dreams, no one would do it for me! I was thirty years old when I finally decided to bounce to the sound of my own drums. I figured that nobody was going to pat me on the back and give me permission to be who I wanted to be or do the things I wanted to do. Ultimately, it was down to me.

If you're still seeking permission to live your best life, let me tell you right now that absolutely no one is going to look at you and say, 'Hey, Amina, can I just say what an amazing mum you are for leaving your kids with your husband to go for a workout at the gym? I'm so proud of you for putting your health first! You go, girl!' Or 'OMG, Noora! Can I just say how inspirational it is to see you creating videos for your blog or writing a paper for your PhD, instead of cooking and cleaning for your in-laws! I wanna be just like you! I'm so motivated by your dedication, sis!'

When you're faced with soul-crushing self-doubt, think of all the Muslimahs you've met. Think about why you admire them. You look up to them and respect them because of the impact they've made on the world, right? But were these women scared? Of course they were! And were they universally admired for fearlessly going after their dreams? No! Of course they weren't! Some got standing ovations, and some were anonymously trolled on the internet.

But all of them felt some fear at one point or another.

The truth is, we all hear those overprotective squeals that cause us to doubt our dreams, and everyone's a little scared to reach for the unexpected and extraordinary. But instead of being crippled by the voice's criticisms, what if we're inspired to stand up stronger, dream harder, work harder? What if we brave it out anyway?

Sadly, I have seen far too many talented women playing small because of their faith. Think of all those dreams not yet lived, all those ideas not yet shared, all those businesses not yet created, books not yet written, movies not yet seen, voices not yet heard, leaders not yet followed, and changes not yet made. All because so many Muslimahs are afraid to close their eyes and go for it, come what may.

Instead of our faith being a reason to excel, we feel that it is a reason not to excel. But look at the Marvellous Muslimahs who dared to dream. They didn't hold back on their ambitions because they were Muslimahs; they pushed through the boundaries *because* they were Muslimahs.

I want this book to help you understand that we come from generations of inspirational dreamers who set the world on fire despite their fears. The question is, what will you do despite yours? We owe it to those great women to not only claim back our legacy but also create new legacies in the process. So, dare to dream. Whatever the goal is, it's yours, no one else's.

Your Turn!

Use the space to write down some of your biggest fears regarding your dreams, and try to think about where the fears are coming from.

When I do this exercise, I write down exactly what I'm afraid of and why I'm feeling that way, and I usually write one or two sentences to reassure the part of my brain that needs to hear that everything is going to be okay. It also helps me to write down a relevant du'a that I can recite every time I feel this way. (sujood.co is a great website to find a du'a for virtually any emotion you're feeling.) My favourite du'a for when I'm feeling afraid: Rabbi aAAoothu bika min hamaza-tiashshayateen. My lord, I seek refuge with you from the whisperings of *shaytaan* (23:97).

The reason I encourage you to name and examine your fears is because the process allows you to look at your fears objectively, do a quick risk assessment, and check if there is any actual validity to your fears.

As you journal your way through this chapter, you'll find your relationship with the negative voice in your head will gradu'ally begin to change. The voice will become quieter and quieter. However, don't become complacent and think that now you've had a crash course on dealing with fear, you're done, because the voice will pop up every time you venture out and try something new. Like Arnold Schwarzenegger's *Terminator*, it'll be brooding in the corner of your mind somewhere, sulking. *I'll be back!*

I am afraid of...

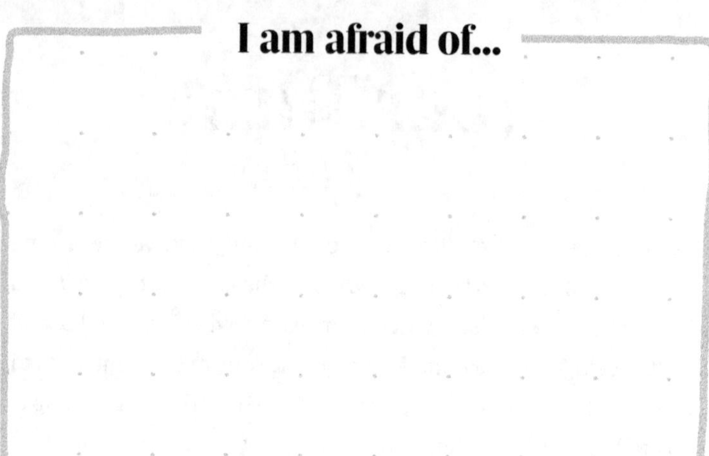

I *feel* this way because...

Don't *worry* because...

My favourite du'a

Meet Nadia Nadim

A Fabulous Footballer

Nadia is an Afghan-Danish professional football player.

Did you know...

→ Nadia is considered one of the greatest female football players of all time. She has scored over 200 goals in her footballing career, and she uses her influence to promote equality for women in sports for the United Nations.

→ Nadia speaks over nine languages fluently and is also a medical student, training to become a surgeon.

"I have one goal in life, I want to be the best, in everything I do."

CHAPTER FOUR

How Thoughts Become Things

In the previous chapter we spent some time exploring several factors that could hinder us from living our best life. We know that some of our influences come from around us, like our upbringing and environment, but we also know that some of it is within us.

We touched slightly on the brain, but that was only the beginning. In this chapter we're going to dig deeper and continue on this magical mystery ride inside the mind and discover...

What does the brain have to do with dreaming big?

I never thought there would come a day when I'd actually regret not taking my science lessons seriously, but here I am, over twenty-five years later, wishing that I focused more when I was being taught the basics about the squishy squashy walnut-shape supercomputer inside my head.

Previously, I vaguely understood that we were either a right-brainer or a left-brainer and it was practically a no-brainer that our DNA and destiny determined how successful we would be in life.

However, science is now telling us that the brain we are born with isn't necessarily the same brain we will be buried with, because just as we grow and evolve through our lifetime, so too does our brain.

Here's the science.

Every single day our brain sends in and out billions of neurons that communicate essential information to the rest of our body. Every time we learn something new, the neurons in the brain develop new connections, and when we repeat the same activity over a certain period of time, these connections strengthen, which means that eventually these connections lead to rewiring the brain.

This phenomenon is known as neuroplasticity, a discovery that suggests the brain is basically like a big ball of Play-Doh.

This really is mind-blowing news because it means that contrary to popular belief, our capabilities are not fixed. Our brain evolves with us as we experience new things, which means we are not confined to our genes, our age, our past, our abilities, or even our destiny. In fact, we can choose to reprogram our brain to become bigger and better, healthier or happier, at any stage of our lifetime.

The brain is endlessly arranging and rearranging its neural pathways to get us through the day. And once the brain gets used to performing a task, it doesn't take long for it to start running on autopilot. Repetition of any task, no matter how hard or complicated, rewires the brain and produces habits.

The more we do something, the more likely it is that the task will become automatic. This means that we need little to no willpower to maintain the new task, and we'll do it with ease again and again in the near future.

Think of all the complicated things you do without ever giving it a second thought. Like ordering pizza on your phone with just your thumb, while watching your favourite show on the telly, while holding a conversation with another person! You can do such things with ease because the tasks are stored in a part of your brain which has figured out how to perform those tasks robotically.

The same goes for thinking: The more we think about something, regardless of whether it is good or bad, the more often it will pop up in your head. The more it pops up, the likelier it is to carve that funky groove in your brain until eventually the thought/belief becomes engraved in your heart and mind, regardless of whether the idea is true or false.

This means that how we think, feel, and act on a regular basis is highly important because, for better or worse, repetition of any thought, emotion, or behaviour rewires the brain and in turn reproduces those thoughts, emotions, or behaviours as habits.

Here's what I really want you to know: If you are not living your dream and you want to do something to change that, the first thing you need to do is change the way your brain works. And to do that, you need to understand how your brain works.

As I delved deeper into this discovery, I also stumbled across the amazing fact that almost all our habits are controlled by the voices heard in our subconscious mind.

Thinking is a bit like blinking. Most of the time we don't even realise we're doing it… unless of course you're seven years old and you're trying to win a staring contest with your best friend.

Whether we're aware of it or not, we spend huge amounts of our day just yapping away to ourselves. We think when we are speaking, listening, watching, reciting, praying, driving, exercising, working, eating, reading. I think the most when I ask my husband what he's thinking, and he says "Nothing"!

The way we talk to ourselves is *waaay* more important than we give it credit for, because our thoughts impact how we act and ultimately dictate the habits that either make or break us.

Our habits are created by the thoughts we've had since we were babies. A scary part is that most of these thoughts aren't even ours—they're actually hand-me-downs that we've blindly picked up through our parents, teachers, the media, and society as well as other voices of authority.

What is even scarier is that our subconscious mind not only goes around eavesdropping on our thoughts about these ideas, values, and beliefs, it also schemes up plans and decides what we should do with the unfiltered information that we take for truths.

But what I find scariest of all is that most of us have no idea that our subconscious mind is calling all the shots! There are so many brilliant Muslimahs out there, going about their day, blowing bubbles out of chewing gum and twerking to inappropriate songs on TikTok, completely oblivious to this life-changing neurological fact.

Everything that happens in, around, and to us impacts the way our beautiful brain develops. This means that the ideas we believe in, the things we see, the sounds we hear, the food we eat, the books we read, the movies we watch, the people we look up to, the company we keep, the emotions we feel, all shape our thoughts, and every single one of those thoughts shapes our lives—positively or negatively.

We create our version of reality with our thoughts.

Therefore, it is incredibly important to guard your mind and to be really intentional about everything you consume, from how much time you spend on devices to who you spend your time with to the types of food you bless your body with, because in the end, they all impact how you think, which in turn impacts your reality.

Your life isn't necessarily happening to you. You are actively constructing it, through your thoughts, every single day.

The more you become aware of this, the more you will become aware of just how powerful your seemingly ordinary, harmless thoughts are. If you truly understand the power of your subconscious mind,

> **The stories we tell ourselves on a daily basis about who we are and what we're capable of are far more powerful than we realise.**

you would think a hundred times about the information you feed it.

Enter RAS.

Our brain is constantly being bombarded with information. Luckily for us, Allah has built in a highly sophisticated network of neurons known as the reticular activating system (RAS), which filters out the unnecessary and repetitive bits of data that are constantly thrown at us, so we can carry on concentrating on the important stuff, like online shopping.

Think of RAS as a friendly concierge who sits at the entrance to your mind. It meets with the voices that want to take up residency in your head and decides who stays and who goes. Depending on whatever you feed your focus on, it's RAS's job to keep that at the forefront of your attention and will keep pointing it out until you have no choice but to acknowledge it.

So, if you find yourself thinking of buying those Chanel shades, chances are your brain will ignore all other brands of sunglasses and will bring only what you're looking for to the forefront of your attention. Suddenly, you'll start noticing Chanel everywhere. You'll see them on other people's faces, or they'll pop up in adverts every time you use the internet. But of course, chances could be that Alexa and Siri have been eavesdropping on your conversations and Google has been tracking your website browsing, which is also why you may find that there's virtually no way of escaping whatever it is you're thinking of.

Now cue LOA (RAS's slightly wilder and more unpredictable cousin).

The law of attraction (LOA) tells us that our innermost, deepest, and most consistent feelings and thoughts are constantly being mirrored back to our reality. It suggests that whether we contemplate at a conscious level or a subconscious level, the thoughts we think carry energy. Huge energy. These thoughts then send a greater wave

We receive what we believe.

of vibration out to the universe, which eventually manifests into something tangible. In other words, our thoughts become things.

The LOA suggests that our thoughts are like magnets. The LOA boomerangs back to us our dominant thoughts and responds to only that which we feed our focus on. It draws in whatever we believe to be true. So, just like those sunglasses you were thinking about, if you're constantly thinking and complaining about how depressing your life is, your brain will seek and point out to you information to support those thoughts.

Only this time, due to LOA, the universe will shift various circumstances and situations to physically bring more things into your life to complain about! When you focus on things you don't want, your brain doesn't hear that you don't want it; it simply manifests whatever you're thinking of.

The same is also true for the opposite. If you believe you will accomplish your lofty goal, the universe will conspire with you to create real possibilities for that to happen.

As I began to realise that my life is a product of my own thinking, I started to make small shifts by removing myself from environments where too many people were filtering out the good stuff and focusing on the bad, whether it was online or in real life. This was by no means an easy task for me.

I mean, positivity and piety are a struggle for me, you guys!

I rarely wake up with bright eyes and jazz hands, singing and dancing, shouting woo-hoo and ready to fist bump my husband and kids. Most days, I wake up grumpy, with achy joints and smelly breath, and as I go through my day there are many occasions when the only time I want to fist bump anyone is on their face!

Although I now understand that unless I choose otherwise, my brain is naturally wired for freak-out mode as a way of protecting me, I didn't always know that. The story I used to tell myself was that I was naturally a Negative Nancy, and I was stuck with it. However, I know now that I'm not the only one, because absolutely everyone is negative by nature and consumed with inner turmoil.

Science tells us that the brain's negative bias is due to an inbuilt alarm system, created by an insane amount of contemptuous chemicals (cortisol) that travel through the bloodstream, causing us to react with panic attacks.

Developmental psychology tells us that there is literally a battle of the brains going on as the higher, more sophisticated part of the brain wants us to grow and evolve whereas the lower, more primitive part of the brain is doing everything in its power to stop us evolving. No wonder we're always stressed out of our heads!

In Surah al Ma'arij (70:19) we are told that "mankind was created anxious". But with patience and prayers we can get out of our own way and overcome our pessimism. The story I tell myself now is that I can change.

I have found that although I may not always have a choice about the (often reactionary and automated) thoughts that whizz through my mind, I can, however, choose the thoughts I want to keep.

In the same way that I won't choose any old thing to match my outfit of the day, I choose my thoughts with careful deliberation to match my outlook for the day.

When you choose your thoughts, you make a conscious decision because you understand that a passing thought can turn into a permanent thought, which turns into an intention, which eventually becomes an action that you do habitually, which eventually becomes a part of your lifestyle, until eventually it becomes a part of your identity.

Your Turn!

Over the years, one of the most powerful ways I have learned to reprogram my subconscious mind to think positive thoughts is through affirmations. Affirmations are basically a bunch of assertive sentences that you use to talk yourself up. I realised that, just as I can build strong habits by repeating an action until it becomes embedded into my identity, I can also repeat strong affirmations to myself until those words represent who I am.

Writing down and consistently repeating my affirmations has been an effective way through which I rewired my brain and regained focus on some of my biggest goals. I hope that they will also help motivate and inspire you to walk closer to your own goals and help you overcome self-sabotaging thoughts and feelings.

Now please don't fill up the writing space with empty "wishful thinking" affirmations. Your brain isn't stupid. Take it from my personal experience that you can't just wake up one day and say, You know what! Screw living like a pauper all the time. I *choose* to believe I've got a million pounds! and suddenly find that someone's mysteriously posted a cheque with a bunch of flowers to you. It just won't work.

The reason it's virtually impossible to magically materialise that perfect body, that perfect job, or that perfect life simply by reciting empty affirmations is because at some point you have to do the work until it becomes a reality.

Here's some others that definitely won't work:

➥ **I'm a money magnet** (Oh, honey, no you're not)

➥ **I look like a Kardashian]** (Girl, stop! Even the Kardashians don't look like the Kardashians!)

➥ **I'm a fajr fanatic** (Seriously? Perhaps you could be, if you didn't stay up on your phone till 2 p.m. every night!)

Focus instead on the qualities and characteristics you might need to achieve your dreams.

Affirmations

Use this space to write down some positive affirmations to help you get closer to your dreams.

I am...

I deserve...

I have...

Meet Nadiya Hussain

A Talented TV Personality

Nadiya is a British Bangladeshi Muslim chef in the UK.

Did you know...

- Nadiya first rose to fame after taking part in *The Great British Bake Off* and has been an award-winning TV presenter since then. She even baked a cake for the Queen's 90th birthday!
- Nadiya uses her voice to be an inspirational advocate for mental health.
- Not only is Nadiya a TV presenter on Netflix and the BBC, she is also a chef, a columnist and has written numerous books.

"I can and I will."

CHAPTER FIVE

Dream Big or Die Trying

By now, you're well on your way to figuring out what you want and why you want it. Now all you need to do is figure out how you're going to get it! The next two parts of this book are all about how you can achieve your wildest dreams, but before we set off, let's get you ready for the journey.

Over the last few chapters, we spent some time exploring the power of our thoughts, where they come from, and why we have them. In this chapter, we'll touch upon how we can transform those thoughts into ways that best serve us.

Dreaming big is a lifelong quest. I can't promise you that you'll reach your desired destination by the end of this chapter, or even by the end of this book, but I can promise you that by the end of it you will know

1. How to manage your mindset

2. How to maintain your mindset

My journey toward dreaming big was a slow process that started with the simple choice of shifting from just *wishing* to achieve my ambitions to *deciding* to achieve my ambitions.

I took my decision to dream audaciously very seriously. I wanted to live a life I could be proud of; I wanted my days to be filled with unlimited love and laughter; I wanted to tick things off my believer's bucket list, one by one. If you're wondering how you can do the same, all you have to do is decide to decide. The moment you begin to change your beliefs, you begin to change your mindset.

A belief is a set of ideas that you value. It could be anything from what or who you worship to what or who you are, to what you can or can't do. Our mindset, on the other hand, is a set of beliefs that has been sewn into our subconscious mind and as a result dictates all our actions and reactions to the world around us.

When you develop a mindset around the belief that you can achieve anything you set your mind to, it doesn't take long to see that belief being manifested into reality. However, when you believe the opposite, your mind goes to work to powerfully prove that this is your truth.

Remember what we learned earlier about the law of attraction? What you think about impacts how you feel; what you feel attracts your reality. I believe it was Ghandi who once said, "Keep your thoughts positive because your thoughts become your words. Keep your words positive because your words become your behaviour. Keep your behaviour positive because your behaviour becomes habits. Keep your habits positive because your habits become your values. Keep your values positive because your values become your destiny".

Whether we like it or not, our mind is constantly churning out self-sabotaging thoughts. As we discovered in previous chapters, it's our mind's warped way of keeping us safe.

These thoughts then have control over our feelings, which in turn have control over our actions and behaviours, which in turn have an impact on whether or not we are successful in achieving our wildest dreams.

As Muslimahs, we have to believe that it's not just our minds that are responsible for all those mean monologues. Sometimes those negative thoughts, or *wiswass* as they are known in Arabic, could also be whispers from jinns, particularly the *shaytaan*, and so we need to seek refuge in Allah, Al Hafeeth, our Protector.

We know this because we are told that negative thoughts can often come from mankind and jinns when we recite the last two *surahs* of the Quran (*Surrah Nas* 114 and *Surah Falaq* 113). We also know this because one of the first things we are taught is to seek protection from these whispers by reciting *al-isti'aathah* (*A'oothu billahi mina-shay-taani-rajeem*) before we begin any task.

Allah teaches us that though we may not be able to control the thoughts that randomly pop up, we do have full control of whether we want to follow those thoughts down the rabbit hole or simply ignore them. Getting rid of negative thoughts is not easy, but with consistent effort it can be done.

If you feel like you are struggling, know that the reason you haven't been able to achieve your dream up until now is because your mindset and habits have been working against you, not for you.

So, how can you manage your mindset?

In chapter 3, I shared three ways of combatting negative thoughts, but on some days when the voice insists on driving me bonkers, I force myself to splash my face with cold water and do *wudhu* so that I can pray my negativity away.

I say "force" because when I'm feeling completely downtrodden and beaten by my own pessimism, I don't feel like talking to anyone, let alone God. (Yes, I know, halal police, I'm the worst! But like I said, positivity and piety aren't my forte—being potty mouthed and pessimistic, however, very much is!)

It takes effort and courage for me to call out to Allah on those days, and I have to work extra hard to push myself out of that funk. But I discovered that the only way to overcome my negative thinking is to occupy my thinking with something else. I try to remember that the thoughts we think are influenced by our environment and that we are what we consume. So I become very intentional about what I let myself think about.

If you want to manage your mindset, be mindful of what you feed your focus on.

The images that we see, the words that we read, the sounds that we hear, all contain subliminal messages that affect us far deeper than we can imagine. Whether the ideas we pick up are true or false, good or bad for us, if we allow them to seep in, they gradually take root and eventually become our mindset.

I also found that one of the best ways to manage my mindset is by reciting from a little book called *Hisnul Muslim*. I'm sure you have one lying around somewhere in the house—we all do!

In Arabic, the word *hisnul* means "fortress" because the book is literally a collection of du'as that can protect us from anything and everything; it is a fortress for the Muslim. Another useful website, which I've mentioned before, is sujood.co. You can type literally any emotion and it will pull up a relevant du'a for you to recite. Try them both; I'm positive they will make a difference to your life too.

Now let's talk about how you can maintain your mindset.

To maintain your mindset, you must be on a constant quest to grow. You must dream big, or at least die trying. We obsess so much over what we wear, which GIFs match our posts, what shade of grey to paint our living room walls, but none of those things matter as much as our mindset. Our mindset is like a pair of reading glasses through which we read our world. If those glasses are scratched and dirty, what is the point of looking through them?

A few years ago, I came across Carol Dweck's important work on the growth versus the fixed mindset, which offers an interesting explanation as to why some people succeed in achieving their dreams whereas others don't. It didn't take long for me to realise that I had a mostly fixed mindset approach to everything.

A fixed mindset is the doom and gloom attitude; it's the belief that our current situation, skills, and abilities are permanent—they can't change and they won't change. The growth mindset, on the other hand, is where we tend to believe that our challenges are exactly that: challenges, exciting puzzles that offer us the opportunity to grow.

For most of my youth I approached my days with a fixed mindset. I told myself ludicrous stories of the things I can and can't do. For example, I'm bad with numbers but good with words, I can't handle fasting but can handle praying, and what's the point in even trying to get fit when I know I'd fail.

It took me a while to get there, but I realised that I was working with a growth mindset when I started to believe that anything I set my mind to could be achieved with consistent energy, effort, and hard work. I was still a perfectionist and hated the idea of failure, but I didn't fear it because I saw myself as a work in progress and I was excited at the potential to learn and improve.

A Muslimah's mindset is always a growth mindset.

Having a growth mindset has allowed me to filter out the positives and focus on them. I totally get that I will never free myself of all the challenges or hardships I'll face in life, and I'm okay with that. This life wasn't designed to be perfect; that's why we call it the *dunya*.

To transform our life, we have to first work on transforming our mind. We have to believe that our creator has blessed us with the abilities that we need to succeed. Remember everything we learned about neuroplasticity? We have to believe that we can do or get better, no matter what it is, how old we are, what our circumstances are, or how privileged we are.

We have to know that our ability to change and improve is flexible, not fixed.

As I went about trying to maintain my new mindset, I found that some days it was easier than others. Some days you will be all high vibe and unstoppable, but other times that voice in your head will remind you of your limiting beliefs and keep you fixed.

What's important is how we handle those hardships, what lessons we take from them, and what we do about them. What's important is to catch yourself when in a fixed mindset, the moment you find yourself heading into a whirlpool of self-doubt and negativity, and train yourself to gravitate toward a growth mindset.

Another mindset that hinders us is the story we tell ourselves about time.

Even when we know what our purpose is, why we want it, and how we're going to achieve it, the greatest lie we believe is that we have time. Lots of time.

I titled this chapter 'Dream Big or Die Trying' because I feel that the greatest disrespect of time is wasting it. In *Surah Asr* (103:1), Allah teaches us that time is precious and the greatest tragedy is that many of us go through life without ever realising the value of time until it is taken away from us.

As a teen I remember hearing advice from the Sunnah, which is to take advantage of five blessings before they are gone: my youth before my old age, my health before it deteriorates, my wealth before I spend it, my free time before I become preoccupied, and my life before my death.

As I leaned more and more toward spirituality, this became one of my favourite reminders. See, the angel of death will not discriminate; death won't care if you're young or old, rich or poor; death won't care about the colour of your skin, the God of your religion, or even what you've posted on your Facebook status.

The only thing Azrael, the angel of death, will care about is that when it's your appointed time to meet with Allah, no matter who you are, where you are, or what your hopes and dreams were, you will not miss that meeting.

In Arabic, the term *akhir* refers as something that is final, something that comes last. Allah describes the hereafter as the *akhira*, the final stage in life. Knowing this, you need to now ask which one of your *dunya* dreams is the final action you can take that will be everlasting enough to take you to your next life, the *akhira*.

I don't want to look back and have the words *I wish* on my lips. I don't want to look back and wish I hadn't wasted my time, wish I'd memorised those *surahs*, wish I'd paid more attention to my kids, wish I'd made more effort with those I love, wish I'd travelled more, or wish I'd hoarded memories instead of things. And I don't want the same for you either.

So, grasp the importance of time before it's too late. Start that blog, launch that podcast, share that idea, stand on stage, memorise that du'a, book that flight, do whatever it takes to get your dream off the ground. Whenever your dreams get lost in the noise, come back to this page to ask yourself this: Are you ready to die without ever having met the greatest version of you?

> **You might not be in control of how you die, but you are absolutely in control of how you live.**

Your Turn!

In this section, you're going to brainstorm your own curriculum for your personal growth. What does that look like for you? Note down some of the things you have fixed views about. What are some of the doubts holding you back from achieving your goals?

Allah Almighty has given us all the resources, tools, and abilities to handle our journey. Our mindset is instrumental to the change we want to see in our lives. The question is, what are you doing to change yours?

Use the following section to shift your fixed mindset to a growth mindset by completing the following sentences.

I've done the first one for you so you can see how easy it is to shift your mindset and look at things from a different perspective.

Use the blank boxes to write about another fixed belief that limits you from achieving your wildest dream. What can you say to counterargue it? But most importantly, what are you going to do about it?

Instead of saying

I can't... (my example: speak Arabic)

Try saying

I am missing...

- ↠ the confidence to speak it
- ↠ the commitment to set aside time to learn the language
- ↠ the tools to learn Arabic

Next steps

People and places that can help me figure this out are...

- ↠ apps

- ↠ Arabic teachers

- ↠ YouTube videos

- ↠ online courses

- ↠ my Arabic friends

Instead of saying
I'm not good at...

Try saying
I'm going to train my mind to...

Next steps
Who or what can help me get better?

Meet Halimah Yacob

A Popular President

Halimah is a Singaporean politician who became the first female president to win uncontested in Singapore.

Did you know...

→ Halimah has been shattering the glass ceiling her entire career. Not only was she the first Malay Muslim woman to become a Member of Parliament (MP), she was also the first female to hold the position of Speaker of Parliament.

→ Halimah came from a humble background and had to skip school to help her mother run her food stall when her father passed away.

→ Halimah studied at the National University of Singapore and graduated with an honours degree in law and continued to pursue her master's and doctorate in law even after she became a successful politician.

"If my life had been a lot easier,
I would not be where I am. But because
my life was tough, that's why I learnt
so many things, I learnt to survive."

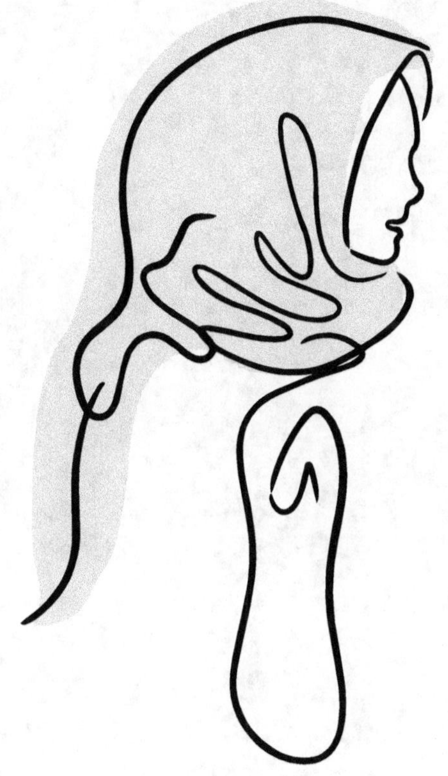

STEP 2:

du'a

CHAPTER SIX

What's Your Why?

Welcome to part two! By now I'm sure that you're sure about your final destination, but you may be wondering how to get there. And so, as we embark on the next part of our voyage and learn about a special superpower called du'a, I want you to think of this section as the preparing stage.

In part one, we answered some pretty big questions:

1. **Who are you?**
2. **Where are you?**
3. **What do you want?**
4. Why do you want it?
5. How are you going to achieve it?

Now, in the second step to achieving your wildest dreams, you will answer the next question—Why do you want it?—and discover that this bit of the book is where the magic really happens!

However, before we go on, I should warn you that it's not all plain sailing from here onward. You may experience some travel sickness, you may have to rethink everything you know about the concept of du'a, and by the time you reach the end you might even need to put a cold flannel on your forehead as we consider a slightly tweaked version of a highly philosophical question once posed by the Spice Girls:

Tell me why you want, what you really really want.

All around the world, billions of believers pray, demand, bargain, or plead to the same God, but every time you've ever felt the need to close your eyes, raise your hands to the heavens, and earnestly whisper your wildest wish to As-Samee, the All-Hearing, it's as if you're the only one in the universe doing so.

This divine gift of connection is a three-letter word known as du'a, and it has the power to change your destiny.

In Islam, du'a isn't just seen as another act of worship, it is seen as the *heart of worship and* our wonderful Messenger said that "There is nothing more noble to Allah the Glorified, than supplication" (Ibn Majah:3829).

There are so many benefits and such beauty from making du'a, and you'll find plenty of *hadiths* and *ayahs* on this topic, but here are my top reasons why it plays such a fundamental part in living a life that I love:

- It is my gateway to Allah's infinite love, mercy, and forgiveness.
- It is my comforter and reminds me that Allah is ever near.
- It is my protector from all things seen and unseen.
- It is the key to accomplishing my wildest dreams.

Du'a is like
the strawberry jam
that glues your "dream"
to the "do".

Without it, everything
will fall apart.

In the following pages, you too will discover why it is the secret to your success, but first, let's check out this funky picture.

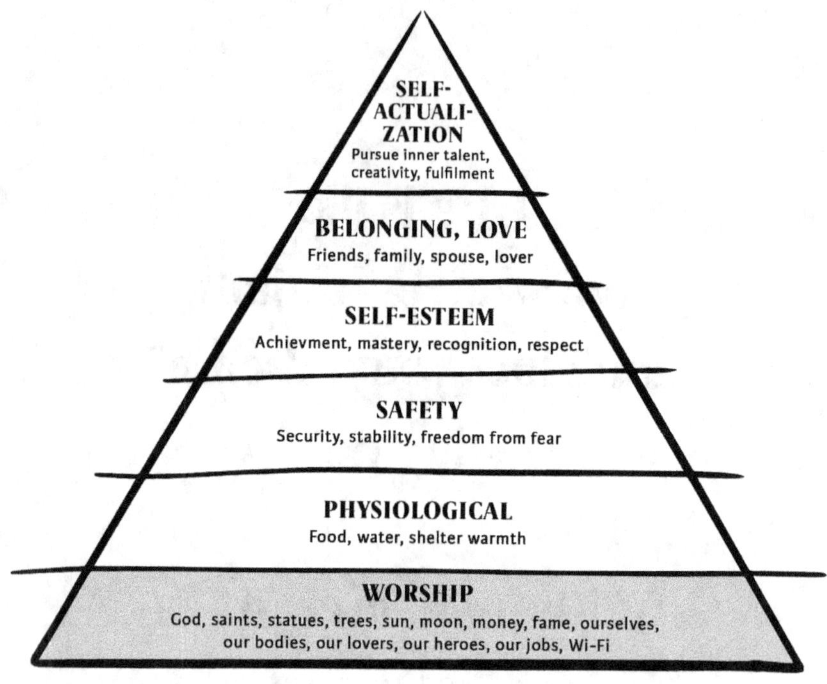

What you're looking at is Maslow's hierarchy of needs. Just in case you've never come across it before, this pretty pyramid is basically the mother of every to-do list you've ever made.

Maslow's hierarchy of needs is useful to understand and apply because it contains all the physiological and psychological needs that must be met for you to not just survive but thrive. Put it this way: Meeting your wildest dreams will not be possible without first checking off the items on this list.

However, as much as I agree with making sure we're well fed and well slept before we even think about dreaming big dreams and self-actualisation, I believe that we have to begin at the very bottom—with what we were all sent down on Earth to do: to worship (which is why I've taken the liberty to scribble it into the hierarchy of needs myself!).

Wanting to worship is innate. It is rooted deep in our nature and has been our most primal need since the beginning of human history. It gives us purpose, a reason to live. It is what drives us, and even if we do try to run away from worshipping God, we end up worshipping something else because it is simply how our brains are wired.

I love the verses in *Surah Al A'raf* (7:172) where we are reminded about a past life when we were gathered in another realm and "Allah asked, Am I not your Lord?" and so we testified the truth that there was no God but God. This pure desire to bear witness to our testament

> **Our mothers may have given birth to us here on Earth, but our souls were born a long time ago.**

is why we search for purpose, because the truth is, we're all looking for something or someone to profess our love to.

In Arabic, this state of utter purity is known as our *fitra*. It is a state that we yearn to return to. This *ayah* teaches me that the reason we can *feel* that God exists is because Allah embedded the memory of this moment in our *fitra*. But, because we're so distracted by the distractions in our daily lives, we become disconnected from our *fitra* and consequently spend our lives trying to fill the void, searching for our way back home, desperately trying to remember what completes us.

If you want to reach your big, lofty goals, you're going to need to meet more than just your physiological and psychological needs. First, you need to meet your spiritual needs.

Du'a is how you get there.

Du'a is a tool and Allah wants you to use it to manifest your wildest dreams. When you recite *Surah al Jumu'ah* (62:10), it tells you to "remember Allah often so that you may succeed". This *ayah* is a reminder that the only way you can truly accomplish something you set out to do is by truly believing that everything you've ever desired is waiting to meet you in *sujood*.

That's when you will realise the greatest truth of all: Du'a was never about Allah, it was always about you.

Du'a is recognising that Allah can and we can't.

When searching for a definition for du'a, I realised that it is more than just an invocation or a supplication. It is about being ever aware of the reality that Allah is Al Ghani, the Self- Sufficient, and needs nothing and no one. But even the strongest and most independent of us still need Allah. We rely on the Almighty for even the smallest things.

Sometimes, some of us forget that du'a is a special gift and so we lose out on this precious opportunity to connect with God. We often think that more showy ways of being Muslim, such as helping each other out with different acts of charity or ranting online about the state of the *ummah*, are far more noble.

Allah wants us to wish for all things wild and wonderful. In *Surah Ghafir* (40:60), Allah Almighty says "Call to me, I will respond to you". This *ayah* teaches us that Allah commands us to make du'a because our Creator knows more than anyone else that our sense of purpose, our reason for being, depends on it.

In a *hadith*, Prophet Muhammad tells us that Allah descends to the lowest heaven and declares "Who is calling Me so I can answer him? Who is asking something of Me that I may give it to him?" (Adab:753).

As a teen Muslimah still trying to figure out my place in the world, both the *hadith* and the *ayah* had a profound impact on me. They helped me realise that Allah is Al Mujeeb, the Responder, and is waiting to guide me and to respond to me. All I had to figure out was what I wanted God to respond to.

The truth is, unless you're one of those rare Muslimahs who always knew what you wanted to be ever since you were born, and literally nothing or no one got in the way of those dreams, most of us don't know what we want to be when we grow up, even when we've grown up. And so we trip, we fall, and we mess up again and again until eventually we figure it out.

Du'a can help us figure it out. All we have to do is raise our hands to the heavens and ask.

Understanding that the reason I was inspired to first make a wish was because Allah had already decided that I deserved what I wished for, was humbling. All I had to do was raise my hands and wish for it.

Perhaps the reason you're reading these words right now is because Allah wants you to call out and make du'a so Allah can respond to your dreams too?

Simon Sinek, who has helped millions find their why, suggests that when your purpose is clear, or when you have a *why*, you have a strong sense of clarity because your *why* acts as a point of reference for everything you do.

The harder you work at forming a relationship with your *why*, the easier it becomes for you to figure out how to achieve your wonderful dreams, and what to do once you get there.

As a Muslim, my *why* is clearly spelled out for me in the Quran and Sunnah. I know that my sole purpose here on Earth is to make God

"

**Our why sits
at the core of who we are
and why we do what we do.**

**It is the reason
we make du'a.**

"

proud enough to allow me a VIP entrance into the Good Place, and so all the du'as I make or any life-changing decisions I take are guided by this *why*.

Whether it was writing this book, moving abroad, completing my master's, having our second child, or performing *hajj*, I knew for sure that that was the dream to pursue at that moment, and so it was easy to connect my du'as to my *why*.

The same can apply for you.

When you remember why you were created and what your purpose is, everything you do from that point forward becomes an act of worship, including going after your dreams. But if you don't make du'a, if you don't remind yourselves *why* you want what you want, you'll never be able to discover your true potential.

> **You will never be able to figure out your what until you figure out your why.**

Your Turn!

Before we head off to the next chapter, use this section to write down your *why*.

It is so important that you take time to connect your dreams to the truth, which is that God wants you to chase goodness. Remember, Allah ordered us to make a wish so it can be given to us.

Whether you want to become a skater like Zahra Lari, a blogger like Vivy Yusof, or a microbiologist like Khatijah Mohammad Yousoff, write down why Allah would want your dream for you.

For instance, if I was writing about my current dream, I would write: *Allah wants me to inspire marvellous Muslimahs to Dream, Du'a, and Do because sharing knowledge is a form of* Sadaqah Jariyah. *It will speak for me long after I have gone and will be the reason WHY I will enter Paradise.*

This affirmation will come to save you, especially on the days your inner critic has highjacked your common sense.

And please don't stop at writing your *why* in the little box that I have kindly provided. Write it again and again with your favourite coloured Post-It notes and stick them all over your house.

Go crazy with them, I dare you. (There's a reason why we Millennials are also known as Generation Y!)

Stick them on all your mirrors, tape them to the back of your TV remote, your kettle, your microwave door. Take a picture of your affirmation and use it as your screensaver. Do what it takes to remind yourself why you're here.

What's your why?

Meet Stephanie Kurlow

A Badass Ballerina

Stephanie is a Russian Australian dancer who is known as the world's first *hijabi* ballerina.

Did you know...

➡ While most two-year-old girls were playing princess with tiaras, Stephanie was already dancing around with her tutu on, dreaming of becoming a ballerina.

➡ Stephanie's identity as a Muslim was important to her and she didn't want to dance without her *hijab*. Unfortunately, there were no ballet schools that were suitable for her, so her mum decided to open a ballet academy for her!

"One day I would like to open my own ballet school that is inclusive of all backgrounds, races and religions, to bring a safe place where all diverse people can come together and create art."

CHAPTER SEVEN

Roadblocks on the Roadmap

What's getting in your way? This chapter is about raising awareness of some of the misconceptions we may have about du'a, and the mistakes we're likely to make. If you want to move forward, you need the blinding belief that Allah's resources are unlimited, and you're also going to have to get rid of some limiting beliefs regarding du'a.

This chapter is about identifying stumbling blocks. Here, we'll take a pit stop to explore the idea that if you are indeed one decision, one action, and quite frankly, one du'a away from turning your dream into reality, then...

What is holding you back?

When I was younger, I'd look at the glamorous lives of the rich and famous and would think that they were living proof that belief in Allah wasn't required for achieving worldly success. Was it the power of the law of attraction that brought them success, or were those thoughts in fact du'as?

I've since come to believe that whether people worship God, the universe, a statue, or even a tree is irrelevant because regardless of how we pray or the name we give to the One we pray to, every single wish of ours sails up to the skies, past the gates of Paradise, to be eventually greeted by the same God.

Allah hears our quietest whispers and our deepest desires, even before we articulate them into du'as, and so Allah, being Ar Rahman, the Most Gracious, never turns us away, regardless of who we are or how we worship.

However, it would also only take me ten minutes of watching *Oprah* to begin to wonder about the stories of the rich and renowned going to rehab to take a break from living their so-called dream lives. On the surface, it seems that their du'as were answered, right? They managed to manifest all the fame, beauty, power, money, success, and accolades in the world, and yet, their du'as failed to fulfil them. Why?

Because their du'as were only half baked.

Allow me to explain what I mean. In Arabic, the word used to describe blessings is *barakah*. When a place, a person, or a purpose has *barakah* you will see unimaginable growth and abundance; its presence can not only be felt but also seen. If you want to know the opposite of *barakah*, the word you're looking for is *lack*.

To have *barakah* in your life, to live in abundance or for your prayers to be powered up to their fullest potential, your du'as must be fully baked with two key ingredients: du'a *al mas'alah* and du'a *al ibadah*.

These are essentially two types of du'a. Understanding them both and incorporating them in your du'a game can change your life radically. I know this because everything I have in my life today is living proof of the power of these prayers.

Du'a *al mas'alah* is the du'a for asking. It's basically when you ask for good things to benefit you in this life, such as '*Ya* Allah, please give me a fancy job so I can buy a fancy car and go on fancy holidays'. Think of it as your *dunya* du'a.

Du'a *al ibadah*, on the other hand, is the du'a of worship. It is making du'a in a practical sense, such as practicing gratitude, seeking forgiveness, reciting your daily *adhkars*, praying, giving charity, fasting, or going on a pilgrimage to *umrah* or *hajj*. Think of it as your *deen* du'a. It is an act of worship that will help you in your *akhira*.

My path to piety began as someone who only knew how to make half-baked du'as: I was only interested in my *dunya* du'as (du'a *al mas'alah*) and just like anything half baked, they failed to rise to their fullest potential.

As a Muslimah born and bred in a Christian country, a common story that I grew up hearing from both faiths was the one about Prophet Adam. But as I got older, it was the story of Iblis (aka Satan) that intrigued me more because when all hell broke loose, Iblis—in his utter helplessness—asked Allah for immortality (du'a *al mas'alah*), but due to his arrogance he completely ignored Allah's commands (du'a *al ibadah*), which is why he was doomed.

The story of Adam and Iblis helped me understand the difference between du'a *al mas'alah* and du'a *al ibdhah*. It had a huge impact on me, and so when I started at university, I decided that to get ahead in life I needed to get better at being a Muslim.

Prior to understanding the difference between the du'as, my relationship with du'a was very shallow. I prayed and fasted because that was what I thought good Muslimahs should do, but there was no sincerity in my haphazard acts of worship. I was only interested in my short-term goals and would often get frustrated if what I wished for didn't come knocking at my door in the way I expected.

For most of my teens to twenties, my *eman* (faith) bounced up and down like a yo-yo, always in a state of fluctuation.

As I blossomed out of my Nokia 3310 days and upgraded to the world of Blackberry (because mankind was still light-years away from inventing the iPhone), I fell in love with the idea of being a Muslimah. I started reading more books on Islam, attending Islamic lectures, praying more regularly, and dressing more modestly.

Before university I had a mix of Muslim and non-Muslim friends. Some smoked, some drank alcopops, but most of us binge-watched *Friends*, obsessed over the way we looked, took loads of selfies, and dreamed of marrying a gorgeous guy. Our priorities were anything but God.

When I entered university, it was all change. I made a conscious effort to make some new holy friends to help me become, well, holier! My new mates were a bunch of halal hippies (minus the dreadlocks and psychedelic music). The boys had long, flowing hair and scruffy beards and carried *tasbihs* in their hands, and the girls floated around in oversized shirts and granny skirts. They *salaam*'ed everyone who crossed their path.

They were all about the *peace, man.*

I wanted so bad to be just like them that I stopped listening to music just in case Satan seeped in through my ears, I lowered my gaze and said *astaghfirullah* if a guy so much as looked at me, and some nights I even contemplated wearing my headscarf to sleep just in case I died in bed and paramedics discovered my corpse!

However, as much as my new friends opened my eyes to Islam as a way of life, I found it hard to keep up with their high horses and low tolerance of anyone who didn't fit into their idea of what a Muslim should look like. I wore a *hijab* on my head, not a halo like them, and the more I struggled to keep up with them, the more I struggled with their version of perfection.

As you can imagine, my inner critic was having a right blast. The more time I spent with my halal crew, the more ashamed I felt for wanting anything materialistic, like better skin, a nicer wardrobe, or eventually a handsome husband. The harder I tried, the easier it felt to believe that I just wasn't good enough. I was constantly fighting my inner monologues about not truly being content with what I had. Because the truth was that I wanted more.

Despite it all, the more I studied Islam the more I realised I had so much more to learn, and it didn't take long to realise that my saintly squad also got the concept of du'a a bit muddled. I realised that, unlike my other friends, my new besties were at the other end of the spectrum. They were Muslimahs who passionately practiced du'a *al ibadah* but ignored du'a *al mas'alah.*

One rainy day in West London, the penny finally dropped. Wearing jeans and a kaftan top that just about covered my bum, I clung on tight to my inside-out umbrella and soggy *hijab* as I obediently followed a group of sisters clad head to toe in flowing black *abayas* to a sisters-only *halaqah* (Islamic study circle).

I was living out my wildest dreams as a self-certified *deen* over *dunya* queen (wild, I know), but as I sat on my prayer mat, I questioned why my journey still didn't feel quite right.

I was working so hard to become an ideal Muslimah, what could possibly be missing?

Sitting on my mat, I realised that even though I was a little girl with big dreams, I was assuming that because I already had so much, I shouldn't ask Allah for anything else. I didn't dare ask Allah for what I truly wanted because deep down, I didn't believe I deserved it or that it could even be already available to me. I couldn't fathom the fact that I was allowed to have more.

Sometimes the biggest roadblocks we come across on our journey to dreaming big aren't created by other people or circumstances. Sometimes we get in our own way because we become too humble for our own good.

You may be doing the same.

What holds us back from making those big du'as is the voice of doubt. When those dreams get lost in the noise of self-doubt, remember that Allah inspired you to recite those words, so seize the blessing you're in because this moment, right here, right now, is an invitation to get closer to your Maker.

Allah has commanded us to make du'a, so watch out for any creeping doubt that makes you feel like you're not a good enough Muslim or too good a Muslim to be praying for whatever your heart desires. Remember that this voice of doubt comes from your own self-sabotaging subconscious or whispers from the *shaytaan.*

So many of us wish for mediocre things, not realising the only restrictions are the ones we put on ourselves. When we make a wish, instead of asking for the biggest or the best, we ask for small, meagre, "realistic" things. We lock our hearts up with limitations and feel too shy to ask, not realising that there is absolutely nothing the Almighty can't and won't do. We forget that what seems impossible to us isn't impossible to Allah. When you raise your hands to make du'a, you are not reminding Allah what your dream is, you are reminding your dream who Allah is.

In a *hadith Qudsi*, Allah says

"Oh my servants, if the first of you and the last of you, and the human of you and the jinn of you were all to stand together in one place and ask of me and I were to give everyone what he requested, then that would not decrease what I possess. Except what is decreased of the ocean when a needle is dipped into it"
(Nawawi40:24).

In another *hadith*, The Messenger of Allah mentioned that

> **"You must not supplicate: 'O Allah! forgive me if You wish; O Allah bestow mercy on me if You wish.' But beg from Allah with certitude for no one has the power to compel Allah". In another narration of the same *hadith* our prophet was said to have said "A supplication should be made in full confidence and one should persistently express his desire (before Allah) in his supplication, for no bounty is too great for Allah to bestow" (Riyadussalihin:1743).**

These beautiful words remind us that the sky is not the limit; we just think it is. Allah's treasure chest is never empty and the only limitations are the ones in our heads. We fail to realise that everything we've ever wanted or everything we've wished of becoming is already right here, right now.

When making du'a you have to firmly believe that nobody but Allah will answer your prayers. Making a half-hearted wish is no good; you need to have absolute, unwavering faith that Allah and only Allah will answer your du'a, and so the best advice I can give you is this:

One of my biggest barriers that blocked my du'as coming to life was that I would make du'a with my head, but deep in my heart I'd already decided that it was unrealistic and therefore unattainable.

When you pray for your aspirations to come alive, make du'a with firm conviction. Don't be wimpy. Don't say things like '*Ya* Allah, I know I won't get through to that job interview, but I'll make du'a just in case I can'. Know that Allah is listening and responding.

In Arabic, having unwavering faith is called *yakeen*. When you have *yakeen*, you act like it has already happened. You need to think, act, and speak as though you already have what you're praying for because when you believe it, that's when you will receive it. Every part of you has to buy in to that belief. When we make du'a, we must have faith

Anything that stops you raising your hands up to Allah is never from Allah.

that whatever we have prayed for has been heard and accepted by Allah Almighty.

When you ask, ask BIG! This is the lord of the worlds we're talking about. Remember in *Surah Yasin* (36:82), Allah simply says "kun fya Kun" be! And it is. Nothing is impossible! Nothing is off limits.

I have practiced both du'a *al mas'alah* and du'a *al ibadah* only to realise that I can't truly live a life filled to the brim with *barakah* (abundance) without both types of du'a intimately intertwined in my daily life. I'm hoping you won't limit yourself by sticking to only one type of du'a.

Here's what I finally figured out: The problem wasn't me making du'a for *dunya* things, the problem was me making du'a just for *dunya* things and neglecting the hereafter. Allah wants the best for us in *deen* and *dunya*. Every du'a *al mas'alah* must contain a du'a *al ibadah* and every du'a *al ibadah* must consist of a du'a *al mas'alah*, because the good you ask for in this world can be a vehicle that drives to goodness in the hereafter.

Your Turn!

When we make a wish, we should ask for our *dunya* as well as ask for the *akhira*. In this section, use the following space to think about how you can incorporate both du'a *al mas'alah* and du'a *al ibadah* to ask for the best of both worlds.

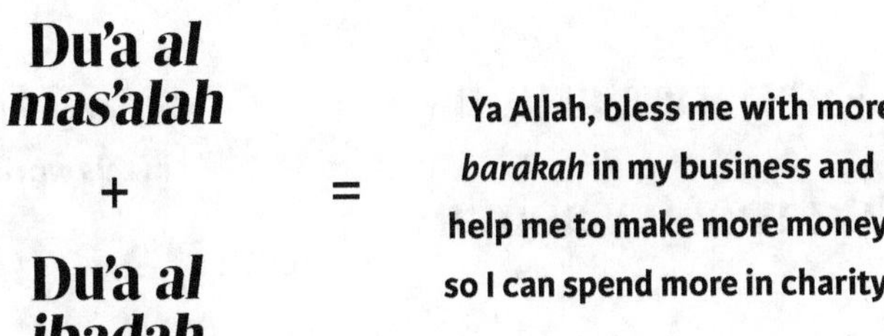

If you find yourself stuck, start by using the following all-encompassing du'a from *Surah Baqarah* (2:201) as a template. This du'a is brilliant because it's asking for the best of both worlds.

Rabbana atina fid-dunya hasanah, wa fil aakhirati hasanah, wa qina adhaban- nar.

Our Lord, give us the good in this world and good in the hereafter and protect us from the torment of hellfire.

Rabbanaa atthina fidunyaa hasanatan

wish for goodness in this world

Wa fil aakhirati hasanatan

wish for goodness
in the hereafter

Wa qinaa azaban naar

and wish for protection
from hellfire

Meet Umm 'Ammarah

A Wonderful Warrior

Umm 'Ammarah was one of the first Muslimahs and was known for her bravery in the battlefield.

Did you know...

→ Nusaybah bint Ka'b, who was lovingly known as Umm 'Ammarah, was a bold warrior-woman who stood up for what she believed in.

→ Umm 'Ammarah is mostly remembered for bravely fighting alongside the Prophet, namely in the battle of Uhud where she protected him from enemies by using her sword and shield.

→ Umm 'Ammarah was of one of the first advocates for the rights of Muslim women and even inspired a verse in the Holy Quran! (33:35)

"I was the only woman to fight in the battle of Uhud."

CHAPTER EIGHT

Did God Just Ghost Me?

Every day, we are given the gift of communication with God. First, we get to hear what Allah has to say through divine revelation in the Holy Quran, and second, we get the chance to have our say when we sit in solitude at the end of our daily prayers. But sometimes it feels like a one-way conversation and we are left wondering if Allah has heard us at all.

This chapter is about investigating why our du'as sometimes seem to be left unanswered and what to do when we feel that Allah is ignoring our prayers. We may come face to face with some uncomfortable truths ahead, so brace yourself for some turbulence as we explore

What to do when du'as don't deliver?

Like me, I'm sure you've had many frustrating moments where you've been making du'a to get that promotion at work or to pass that test, but you're still not catching your lucky break. You may be wondering what's going on. You may be wondering why your du'as are not being answered.

Before we answer that question, let's take a minute to think about the purpose of that particular du'a you're making. What are you actually wishing for?

Sis, in my experience, if your du'a hasn't come to fruition despite months or even years spent making du'a for a particular dream to come true, maybe it's time to take a closer look at the du'a itself.

Maybe some of my du'as were not answered in the way that I wanted because I confused my means with my end.

See, our end is our big lofty dream of entering Paradise, whereas our means is the vehicle we use to get there. When we confuse our means with our end, our du'as are not always answered in the way we want because what we're making du'a for isn't going to help us with our endgame.

I'm sure you've got yourself some smashing goals, but the simple truth is that as Muslims, aside from pleasing our Almighty, the Most High, and earning those *Jannah* points, everything you make du'a for needs to be aligned with that ultimate dream of Paradise.

Imagine you have a friend who wants to marry a handsome revert she met while volunteering at her local charity project. While working with him, she got to know him and now she's madly in love, utterly besotted. Although Islam loves interracial marriages, her father, still clinging to how things worked "back home", sees it differently. 'I don't get it,' your friend says, 'I've been praying for so many months for my dad to have a change of heart and let me marry him, but he just won't budge in his decision. He wants me to marry my cousin instead!'

What would you say to her?

You may feel sorry for her and give her a massive hug, or you might remind her to love the Creator not the created because it's as clear as day to you that her desperado du'as had nothing to do with her *deen* but everything to do with her *dunya*.

As painful as it is watching your friend not get what she wishes for, what if the answerer of that du'a knows that her idea of Mr Right is oh so wrong for her? What if she's so besotted with her potential partner that her focus is *only* on him, her happiness depends on him, and consequently her highs, her lows, her everything is attached only to him, not Allah?

Now, imagine if she switched her du'as round a bit and asked Allah to be wed only if it was good for her in her relationship with Allah, if it was good for her in *deen* and *dunya*. If she'd done that and still didn't get what she wanted, she probably wouldn't be so heartbroken, would she? (I mean, she might have to eat a few tubs of ice cream and watch *Titanic* a couple of times, but in the end she'd get over it because she knows the marriage wasn't right for her.)

In our limited understanding of our destiny, we forget that the reason we become frustrated when we don't get what we want is because we're not always interested in investing in a relationship with Allah. We are far too invested in ourselves.

> **What if that du'a you've frantically been making doesn't get you closer to Allah?**

Allah wants us to ask for what we want, but when we make the things we want the *goal*, we need to question our intentions for making that du'a.

Sometimes we get so fixated on our dreams that we don't pause to ponder whether they are good for us. We become so obsessed with getting what we want that we never stop to consider whether this thing we want could in fact be bad for us.

I love the verse in *Surah Baqarah* (2:216) where Allah Almighty says

"Perhaps you would hate a thing while it is good for you; and perhaps you would like something that is bad for you, Allah knows, and you know not".

This verse lovingly tells us that Allah knows us better than we know ourselves. Sometimes we think that something or someone is good for us, although it is the opposite, but because we're so consumed with achieving that goal, we become obsessed with only the dream and forget about our wider dream, our ultimate purpose in life.

Wherever you are in your journey to dreaming big, know this: Allah always, *always* knows what's best for us. We need to remember that our worldly pursuits, such as our accomplishments or accolades, our business successes or relationship status on our socials, are not in themselves our purpose. They are a means that lead us to our true purpose.

Another big reason why you may not be seeing your prayers come to life could be down to your beliefs and attitudes regarding the du'a you

Du'a isn't like placing an order on Amazon Prime.

make. Once, when sitting amongst his companions and talking about the concept of making du'a, our Prophet Muhammad said "It is necessary that you do not become hasty". A companion asked "What does being hasty mean, O Messenger of Allah?" He answered "When one says: 'I supplicated to Allah but Allah did not answer me'" (Ibnmajah:3853).

The du'a of a believer will surely be answered, so long as we don't get antsy and give up at the first hurdle.

When we order something over the internet, we usually get what we paid for, but when we make du'a we make zero contributions financially, so ideally, we should walk around with zero expectations spiritually; we have no right to complain about what we get.

If you've made du'a and still not received your gift, know that it is for your own protection. It is out of Allah's love and mercy for you that Allah has withheld what you wanted, and no doubt you'll be rewarded with something far better. Remember that *ayah* we talked about from *Surah Baqarah* (2:216) and learn to love the fact that good things take time.

For a long time, I didn't get that it was Allah's timing, not my timing, that was perfect. This was the one thing about du'a I struggled with the most. I could quite happily sit through an entire series on Netflix just because someone told me it gets good in season three, but I struggled to find the patience to persevere with my prayers.

If you're feeling a little impatient right now, remember you will achieve your dreams at whichever age or whatever stage you are meant to. Remember all those amazing Muslimahs you've met?

Dalia Mogahed became the first Muslim woman to advise the White House in her mid-thirties. Malala Yousofzai became the youngest person to win a Nobel prize at the tender age of seventeen. Halima Yacob became the first Muslim and first female president of secular Singapore at age sixty-five. They didn't get to where they got to in their time; they got to where they got to in God's time.

If you do find that the single most important reason you want to pursue your passion is just fame or fortune (or a man), you need to go back to your favourite cafe, order yourself a cappuccino, and think long and hard about what you really want out of this one-time opportunity called your life.

Allah always
answers our du'as.
Your job is to be open
for when that
happens.

Your Turn!

In this section, I want you to reflect on a *hadith*, where our lovely Messenger said "There is not a man who calls upon Allah with a supplication, except that he is answered. Either it shall be granted to him in the world, or reserved for him in the Hereafter, or, his sins shall be expiated for it according to the extent that he supplicated—as long as he does not supplicate for some sin, or for the severing of the ties of kinship, and he does not become hasty" (Tirmidhi:3604d).

Use the space to think of reasons your du'a hasn't been delivered to you yet. Is your *dunya* dream connected to your *deen*? Is the end goal of your du'a to get closer to God? Is the du'a asking for something that is halal and good for you? Or have you been row, row, rowing your boat gently down the stream with the wrong end of the stick?

Have you confused your end with your means?

I want you to leave this section feeling confident that whatever it is you wished for, Allah the All-Hearing has heard you, but just because it's been heard doesn't necessarily mean you will get what you want when you want or in the way you want. The outcome of your du'a can manifest in several ways:

➻ It can be answered straight away
➻ It can be reserved for you later
➻ It can be replaced with something better

Accept that you might not always get exactly what you asked for. Allah hears all your du'as, but in infinite wisdom also sees the bigger picture. Allah is omniscient and knows best if what you are asking for is good for you or not.

There is a certain sweetness to patiently waiting on a prayer. The longer you pray, the longer you stay connected to God. So be persistent and keep dreaming big because your time will come.

Eventually, when you look back and reflect on all the du'as that still haven't been manifested, you will see that it's highly possible that by you not being where you thought you should be, you're exactly where you're meant to be.

Brainstorm reasons why your du'a hasn't been answered yet

Meet Jawahir Roble

A Remarkable Referee

Jawahir is Somali British and is the UK's first female Muslim football referee.

Did you know...

→ Jawahir was just ten years old when she escaped the civil war in Somalia to move to London with her family.

→ Jawahir has always loved playing football and as a child her big goal was to become a professional football player. However, it wasn't a dream her family was keen on. So instead of giving up football altogether, she set her sights on becoming a football coach and refereeing.

→ Jawahir is an inspirational role model for young girls who want to participate in a sport that is typically considered a man's sport.

"One day I would like to officiate in the Premier League."

CHAPTER NINE

Questioning Qadr

In Arabic, the word *qadr* refers to predestination or fate. It is a concept that plays a big role in a Muslim's belief system, but the word is often misunderstood. I've lost out on many precious opportunities to wish for my wildest dreams because I convinced myself that a good Muslimah shouldn't question *qadr*, that my future was God's business, not mine. I'd hate for you to make the same mistake.

In this chapter we will discover a magical prayer that has the potential to change your life. Come with me as we ask

Can du'a change my destiny?

I am the eldest daughter on both my maternal and paternal sides, and since my cousins and sister still had a good couple of years ahead of them before they could even be considered marriage material, I was the first in line.

My family couldn't wait to have their first ever big fat Bengali wedding. It was one of my parents' biggest dreams as well as one of mine, and so the idea of marriage was introduced to me at the ripe old age of fifteen!

I am a second-generation Bengali, born in the UK. This means that we are that awkward generation where we're not quite Bengali but not fully English either. We were the first to challenge tradition, the first to make our mark on the internet, the first to question our place in our community, and so, being a Millennial, I was the first in my family to consider another option other than getting married off and living happily ever after.

I laugh now as I remember going on a holiday to Bangladesh, where my nanu (maternal grandmother) introduced me to not one but two grooms to choose from simultaneously. Yep, you read right, two for the price of one, baby!

Sixteen years old. Dressed awkwardly in a sari, I shuffled into my grandmother's living room, not knowing what to expect. I knew I was to have an arranged marriage, but what I didn't expect to see were two brothers sitting nervously with their hands on their quivering knees like a couple of blushing brides. Their family was sitting beside them, eager for me to pick.

I laughed even harder about a year later when my dad excitedly invited another would-be groom to our house, a nice young chap he met in the local *masjid*. My dad's never been a man of many words, nor does he get overly excited about anything, so it meant a lot to me when he said, 'This one is a very good boy, but he's a little bit healthy.'

My intention is not to fat shame at all, but it turned out that this guy was so damn "healthy" he literally had to walk sideways to get through the living room door!

Sadly for my parents, I let another great groom slip away that night.

Just so we're clear, Bengali brides are meant to modestly blush their way through these awkward meetings, not burst into fits of giggles.

But when everyone around you thinks that they have found the "one" for you, and you offer samosas to a dude who just about comes up to your shoulders, what else could I do but laugh.

These incidents will make great bedtime stories to tell my grandchildren one day, but when you're an eighteen-year-old being forced to make a very scary decision whilst dolled up and serving tea to complete strangers, it can be a daunting experience.

Especially if you throw someone like me into the mix. I can't even decide what the heck to eat for breakfast or what to wear just to go to the local supermarket.

It was right when my parents started thinking it was time to marry their first daughter off that I stumbled across a magical du'a called *al istikhara*.

This special du'a is often recited to request divine guidance. The first time I came across it, my face morphed into that shocked emoji, all wide eyed, hands on my mouth. *OMG!* I thought, *why didn't I know about this before?* It made me question everything I knew about *qadr*.

Prior to discovering this du'a, I used to think that everything in my life was prewritten, hence my bleak attitude. If my fate was already sealed with a loving kiss, down to the finest detail, what was the point of me even asking of making du'a *al mas'alah* and wishing for big, audacious things?

However, all that changed when I came across a famous *hadith*:

"Nothing repels the Divine decree except supplication" (Ibnmajah:4022).

This *hadith* made me realise that nothing can change the divine decree except du'a. Although it is true that our fates are prewritten, with the power of prayer, it can all be rewritten!

Mind, blown.

A year later, a marriage was finally arranged for me, and I reluctantly got engaged.

I was well into the first year of uni and my family were debating with my future in-laws whether I should give up my studies or continue after the wedding. Sociology was a useless degree anyway, better to be realistic, settle down, and get the kids out the way while I'm young, I was told.

Nineteen and naïve. Now, posing for the camera and cutting a cake with my fiancé next to me, I wasn't laughing anymore. Prior to this engagement party, I had turned down countless grooms, and much to my parents' distress, it was becoming a sore topic in my house. Getting married was an important dream for my family, and being the people pleaser that I was, I didn't want to be a party pooper and let everyone down.

At that time, my only dream was to finish university, but everyone else had other dreams for me. My mum and aunts all got married and had children at ages that still make me feel nauseous, and all the girls around me got married before they hit the Jurassic age of twenty, so it only made sense that I should do the same.

And so there I sat, my prayer mat and me.

I still remember that moment when I recited the *istikhara* du'a in floods of tears, feeling confused and stuck at a crossroads. Maybe my parents knew what was best for me, maybe dreaming of graduating was a dumb idea; after all, it's not like I knew what I wanted to do with my life after that.

And so I prayed, taking my time and meaning each part of the *istikhara* du'a that I uttered in prayer. '*Ya* Allah, if this is good for me then bless it for me and remove all obstacles out of the way, but if this is bad for me, by some miracle take me out of this situation without me bringing shame to me or my family.'

I desperately needed some divine intervention.

Soon after, even though the date had been fixed, my outfit chosen, the venue booked, and the preparations well under way, the wedding was abruptly cancelled! I want to conjure up a scandalous story about why the engagement broke off, but the simple truth was that the groom and I were incompatible. We didn't even fancy each other, and so he made the brave decision to call it off.

My family mourned the death of my wedding as if I had become a widow. All I needed was to put on a white sari like they do in those Bollywood films and break the glass bangles on my wrists as I banged on the wall, wailing about the tragedy that had befallen me! But as I left for uni that day, I glanced over at my mum ranting on the phone to an aunt about my cancelled wedding, and I smiled, knowing that *istikhara* had just changed my destiny. I felt like a survivor from a Hollywood movie, walking away from an inferno of explosions.

Now, as someone reading my (slightly embellished) story

twenty years later, you may not be having to choose between going to uni or getting married. But I am totally sure that you too have faced a decision or two where you could have used some divine guidance.

Up until I discovered *salatul istikhara*, I hadn't been aware of this awesome decision-making process that could hold my hand and guide me along my skittish ways.

I've had to go through some pretty ugly times to truly appreciate the beauty of the *istikhara* du'a. I have learned that whenever I have made this du'a, it has taken on a life of its own and become the custodian of my dreams.

Praying *salatul istikhara* sparked my curiosity about the power of prayer, and I began to wonder what other du'as were out there that could help me in other aspects of my life. What else could I do to manifest what I want through du'a?

I hope it sparks your curiosity too.

Your Turn!

Now that you've received a crash course on *salatul istikhara*, I want you to have a go at asking for divine guidance.

The beauty of *salatul istikhara* is that it teaches you the subtle art of letting go.

Once you make that du'a, observe without judgement. Be pragmatic. Don't expect any lightning bolts or fireworks. It's magical, but not in a unicorn and rainbow kind of way. Instead, expect that Allah will shift circumstances and people around you to guide you to what is meant for you.

All you have to do is pray.

Consider *salatul istikhara* as a delish three-course meal.

The first part of this meal is the starter, so start by making a clear intention of praying the *istikhara*. You don't need to say it out loud and you don't need to write a fancy poem to God either; simply take a deep breath and think about the issue you're asking Allah guidance for.

The second part of your meal (the main) consists of praying two *raka'at*. You'll begin by announcing the *takbeer* then follow each *rakah* with *Surah Fatiha* and another *surah* of your choice. As you pray the two *raka'at*, stay focused on what you want Allah to help you with, and turn toward Allah in humility and total submission.

And third, the part of the meal you've been looking forward to the most: dessert!

It was narrated that our Messenger used to teach his Companions to perform *istikhara* in all sorts of matters and stated that "If any one of you is deliberating about a decision he has to make, then let him pray two Rak'ahs of non-obligatory prayer, then say:

Allahumma inni astakhiruka bi 'ilmika wa astaqdiruka bi qudratika wa as'aluka min fadlika, fa innaka taqdiru wa la aqdir, wa ta'lamu wa la a'lam, wa anta 'allam al-ghuyub. Allahumma in kunta ta'lamu anna hadhal-amra khayrun li fi dini wa ma'ashi wa aqibati amri faqdurhu li wa yassirhu li thumma barik li fihi. Allahumma, wa in kunta ta'lamu annahu sharrun li fi dini wa ma'ashi wa 'aqibati amri fasrifhu 'anni wasrifni 'anhu waqdur li al-khayr haythu kana, thumma radini bihi.

(O Allah, I seek Your guidance (in making a choice) by virtue of Your knowledge, and I seek ability by virtue of Your power, and I ask You of Your great bounty. You have power, I have none. And You know, I know not. You are the Knower of hidden things. O Allah, if in Your knowledge, this matter (then it should be mentioned by name) is good for me in my religion, my livelihood and my affairs (or: both in this world and in the Hereafter), then ordain it for me, make it easy for me, and bless it for me. And if in Your knowledge it is bad for me and for my religion, my livelihood and my affairs (or: for me both in this world and the next), then turn it away from me and turn me away from it, and ordain for me the good wherever it may be and make me pleased with it) (Nasai:3253).

All you have to do is pray.

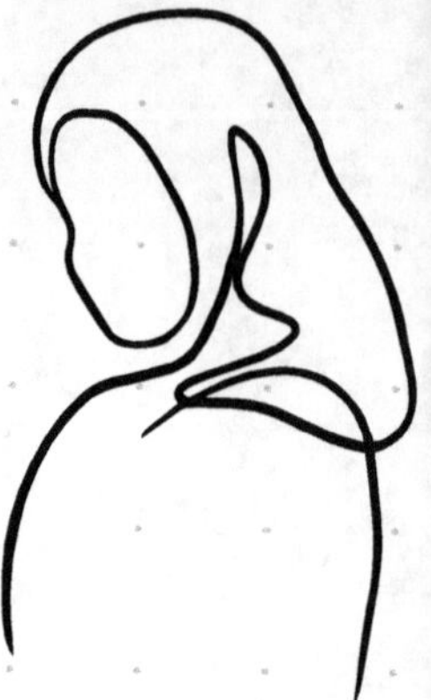

Meet Muniba Mazari

An Awesome Activist

Muniba is a Pakistani activist. She is the first wheelchair-using model and singer, and a motivational speaker.

Did you know...

- Muniba is known as the Iron lady of Pakistan and is the survivor of a car accident at the age of twenty-one. Despite the doctors telling Muniba that she would be completely paralysed from the hips down, Muniba refused to become a victim of her circumstances. Instead, she used her adversity as an opportunity to empower other women and has been continuing to do so ever since.
- Muniba has achieved so much over the years, she has

  - appeared in the BBC's "100 Most Inspirational Women in 2015"
  - appeared in the Muslim 500
  - appeared in a TED talk inspiring so many women
  - appeared in a 30 under 30 Forbes list in 2016
  - become the national ambassador for UN Women Pakistan

"We came with nothing, we'll leave with nothing, it's what we do in between."

CHAPTER TEN

The Art of Making Du'a

In the past, it was safe to say that my du'as lacked a little lustre. They were floppy and sloppy and I struggled to articulate what I really wished for. I would resort to reciting a couple of partially memorised du'as that I barely understood the meaning of, and as a result failed to see any major shifts in my life.

You too may find that even though you now know the importance of connecting your dreams with du'as, something is still missing.

Du'a can accelerate your life to a whole other level, but to do that, you need to know the tricks of the trade. In this chapter we will do two things: First, we'll learn how to craft an effective du'a that is specific to our dreams, and next, we'll explore how to make du'a. It's going to be a very busy chapter, so brace yourself as we explore

What is the secret to a really good du'a?

Du'a is a verb. It's a doing word.

As a young Muslimah in my early twenties, I didn't understand this concept and found that making du'a wasn't as easy as I would have liked. It took a whole lot of practice as well as patience; in fact, it took me years to truly appreciate the art of making du'a. If I could go back in time to whisper in my ear (in a non-creepy way), I would tell myself this: If you make lame du'as, you'll get lame results. Fact.

Raising your hands and saying a sloppy '*Ya* Allah, grant me success' is a bit like wandering around with a blindfold on and taking a shot in the dark. If that's your version of shooting for the stars, go ahead, but I can assure you that you won't shoot very far. I know this because for a while, I didn't go very far.

If you want success, you need clarity on what that looks like and what it feels like, and you won't be able to experience either if you don't articulate those words into a du'a.

In chapter 7 we started to explore crafting our own personal du'as by using both du'a *al mas'alah* and du'a *al ibadah*. We used a du'a from *Surah Al Baqarah* (2:201) as a template to help us create our own du'a that will serve a purpose in this world and the next.

But now it's time to give that du'a an upgrade.

The next step to turning your dreams into awesome du'as is to make sure that they are SMART. Crafting a really gorgeous du'a is about making sure it is specific, measurable, actionable, relevant, and timely. If you create SMART du'as, it means you know exactly what you want, why you want it, and what you're going to do about it.

Specific: For your du'as to manifest in the ways that you want, they need to be tangible, and for them to be tangible, you need to get hyper specific. For example, instead of saying '*Ya* Allah, bless me with a nice husband', be specific. What is your idea of a nice husband? What are some of the characteristics you want in him that makes him a nice husband?

Measurable: A good du'a should be measurable. Don't say '*Ya* Allah, make me rich'. That's too vague. Give God some numbers to work with! How rich do you want to be? Do you want to be rich enough to pay off your student debts, do you want to be rich enough to retire in the Bahamas someday, or just rich enough to buy the next Dior handbag?

Actionable: Okay, this is important. We can't afford to be wishy-washy. If your du'as can't help you take real solid actions toward your dream, I'm afraid all you have is just words. What actions do you need to take to make your dream come true? Use du'a to ask for wisdom, courage, strength, finance, or whatever else you need to take action-able steps to achieving your goal. For instance, if I want to get fit, I wouldn't say '*Ya* Allah, help me become healthier'. Instead of saying '*Ya* Allah, help me lose weight' or '*Ya* Allah, help me get fit', I would say '*Ya* Allah, help me commit to twenty minutes on the treadmill a day for the next six months'.

When you switch your du'as to being behaviour orientated, they become daily reminders not for God but for you to pursue. They become actionable.

Relevant: A good du'a is not only relevant to your *dunya* but also to your *deen*. If you have forgotten the purpose of chasing that big audacious dream, go back to your *why*. Why do you want to achieve your wildest dream? What is the objective? And how does it link to your ultimate goal of attaining *Jannah*?

Timely: Obviously we know that Allah's timing is perfect, and obvi-ously I'm not saying that we should expect to make a du'a on Monday and have it delivered on Friday, but in my experience I have found that when I gave myself a deadline, it got me moving. The moment you put a deadline on your dream, it becomes a goal. So, if one of your dreams is to start driving, don't be afraid to say '*Ya* Allah, help me pass my driving test by next month'. The rest is up to Allah.

Congratulations! You've managed to carve out a wonderful du'a that is very specific to your dream. You go, girl! You're halfway there!

Now all you need to do is sit down and make that du'a so your wildest dream can come true. Sounds straightforward, right?

Wrong!

Du'a is an act of worship, which means that just as we can't use our imagination to decide what is *haram* or halal, or go rogue on the rituals we perform for *salah*, Ramadan, or performing *hajj*, we can't decide how to make du'a according to our own whims and desires. The Quran and Sunnah tell us that when it comes to making du'a, there are certain rules of etiquette to follow.

I used to skip this part because it required time and effort to follow all the rules and regulations. I just wanted to fast forward to the bit where my dream became reality. As I've gotten older, I've realised that these rules were in fact the secret to achieving my wildest dreams; they were a form of art.

If you're hoping for a couple of your du'as to be answered, you're going to have to put in the time, effort, and energy too.

Obviously, having the basics of being a Muslim covered, such as testifying to the *shahadah*, praying *salah*, paying *zakat*, fasting, and performing *hajj* can give you a good head start. And when it comes to the actual practice of making du'a, being in a state of cleanliness (in *wudhoo*), facing the *qibla*, and sitting in the *tashahud* position when making du'a can all help keep you focused psychologically as well as spiritually.

But if you really want to amplify your du'a-making game, here's something you might want to consider with a fizzy drink and extra-large side of fries.

Believe it or not, the secret recipe to making a really good du'a is to imagine it as a big fat juicy burger. Bear with me on this. I promise it will all make sense once I'm done introducing you to the McDu'a.

The art of making du'a is imagining the process as something that consists of several layers.

1. **The first layer is your base, so start off strong on this one.**

    This means that you begin the du'a-making process with sincerity and humility. Mention your helplessness and dependence on Allah, praise Allah by reciting **laa hawla wa laa quwwata 'illlaa billaah** (there is no power and no might except Allah), and most importantly, ask for forgiveness (*istighfar*).

    When you recite *astaghfirullah,* or recite any other prophetic du'as seeking *istighfar*, it prepares your subconscious mind to let go of any self-sabotaging thoughts that are holding you back from chasing your wildest dreams. We know that our Creator is Al Ghaffar, the Most Forgiving, and so when you accept that Allah has forgiven you, it becomes easier to forgive yourself.

2. **The second ingredient in your burger is the cheese.**

This bit glues your du'a together. In a *hadith*, we are told that a believer's "supplication stops between the heavens and the earth, nothing of it is raised up until you send salat upon your prophet" (Tirmidhi:486).

Therefore, one of the most basic etiquettes of making du'a is to begin with sending peace and salutations upon our Prophet by reciting **Alahumma salli 'ala Muhammad wa 'ala ali Muhammad, kama sallaita 'ala Ibrahima wa barik 'ala Muhammad kama barakta 'ala ali Ibrahim fil-'alamin, innaka hamidun majid** (O Allah, send *salah* upon Muhammad and upon the family of Muhammad, as You sent *salah* upon the family of Ibrahim).

3. **The third part is the meat.**

This is the bit where you get to make it really juicy by asking Allah for what you want, so don't be afraid to repeat your du'as here (at least three times). The magic in this part is in the vocabulary you use. In *Surah Al A'raf* we are told that "the most beautiful names belong to Allah" (7:180), so call out to Allah using the names inspired in the Quran, all ninety-nine of them.

When we remember Allah using the ninety-nine names, we develop a deeper appreciation of God because we are mindful of all the powerful attributes. This will inevitably lead you to loving Allah even more than you already do.

Each name of Allah has a specific purpose. You will find that when you pray with purpose you will begin to live with purpose. It's only when you're mindful of the attributes of God that you will see manifestations happening around you.

My biggest difficulty with making du'as stemmed from the fact that I couldn't make an emotional connection with God. I couldn't figure out why then, but now it seems so obvious: I couldn't because I knew so little of our Creator.

The key to making a connection with God is through knowing the names of Allah so well that you have a personal relationship with each name. For example, if you are waiting for a certain window of opportunity to open, say '*Ya* Allah, you are Al Fattah, the Opener...' Be excessive in your praise for Allah. Say **La hawla wa la quwatta illa billa** (There is no might but Allah).

When making your main du'a, remember to use the template we discussed in chapter 7. Ask for good in this world and the hereafter, and connect your du'a to both.

4.   **The fourth ingredient is your lettuce and tomatoes, your add-ons, so here you might want to recite your favourite du'as from the Quran and Sunnah.**

Here are a few good ones:

Du'a of Prophet Ibrahim (14:41)

Our Lord! Forgive me and my parents, and the believers on the Day when the judgement will come to pass

Rabbana ighfir lee waliwalidayya walil-mumineena yawma yaqoomu alhisabu

Du'a Prophet Musa (20:25–28)

O my Lord! Uplift my heart for me. And make my task easy; And untie the knot from my tongue, so people may understand my speech

Rabbi ishrah lee sadree Wayassir lee amree Waohlul AAuqdatan min lisanee Yafqahoo qawlee

Du'a of Asiya(66:11)

My Lord, build for me near You a house in Paradise

Rabbi ibni lee AAindaka baytan fee aljannati

If Arabic isn't your first language, use the translations to learn what you're reciting because what good are those du'as if you don't know what you're asking for? When I think about the times I used to rock back and forth, regurgitating some poorly pronounced Arabic words I barely understood, it makes me cringe! I may as well have recited lyrics to a K-pop song; it would have had the exact same effect.

5. **Fifth, because we're going all out, we'll add a dollop of our favourite sauce, so once again dollop peace and salutations on our Prophet as well as praising Allah to make your du'a really stick together.**

6. **And last, the top bun.**

Seal your du'a with having absolute *yakeen* in the fact that your du'a has been answered. Top it off with a profound du'a made by Prophet Yunus:

We are told in a *hadith* that whoever recites this du'a, their wishes are never ignored.

Our Prophet said that no one "supplicates with it for anything, ever, except Allah responds to him" (Tirmidhi:3505).

Finish up with gratitude, by reciting *alhamdulillah*. And say *ameen*. Whatever you do, don't be a Hasty Halima and be impatient over the acceptance of your prayers.

I heard once that du'a is a bit like taking medicine; consider it your daily dose of vitamin *deen*. And although taking them as and when you

There is no du'a too big or too small for Allah to make reality.

like can be beneficial, Allah has prescribed better times or ways they need to be consumed in order to give our du'as the greatest chance to nourish us. Therefore, the art of making du'a also involves taking advantage of the recommended times and places.

Surely there isn't a magical, mystical twilight time where all our wishes come true? I hear you ask. Well, now that you've mentioned it, there is, and it's called *tahajjud!*

Tahajjud is a voluntary prayer usually performed in the last portion of the night and is a very powerful, spiritual time to make a wish. Our beloved Prophet said "The most excellent prayer after that which is obligatory is the (voluntary) late night prayer" (Bulugh/2/273).

It is said about *tahajjud* that "Our Lord descends every night to the nearest heaven, until the last third of the night remains, so He says: 'Who is calling upon Me so that I may answer him? Who is asking from Me so that I may give him? And who is seeking forgiveness from Me, so that I may forgive him'" (Tirmidhi:3498).

Imam Ash Shafi'i was also reported to have said "the du'a made at *tahajjud* is like an arrow that does not miss its target". I love that quote. Most of the great things I have been gifted were a result of me raising my hands high up to the heavens when the world around me was sleeping.

If you want to achieve your wildest dreams, then I suggest you wake up for *tahajjud* too, because let's face it, you can't claim that you've done everything to make your dreams come true if you haven't done *tahajjud!*

The art of making du'a lies in the art of taking advantage of moments like *tahajjud.* There are lots of other times that you can maximise the power of prayers too.

Here are some more.

Fridays (Jumu'ah)

Ashurah

At the end of Fard prayers

Rabi al awwal

27th Rajab

Between the iqamah and the adhaan

15th Sha'ban

Laylatul qadr

Tahajjud—the last third of the night

The days of Eid

When it rains

In sujood

1st ten days of Dhul Hijjah

Day of Arafah

Ramadan and when fasting

When drinking zam zam water

When travelling

When in umrah/hajj

Essentially, the secret to the art of making du'a consists of three key ingredients.

First: the audacity to dream bigger, to wish things for yourself without any limitations holding you back. Allah wants us to dream, in fact, the bigger the better.

Second: a slightly wacky du'a. If it was easily achievable you wouldn't be needing to call out to Allah, would you? Aim for something a bit out of reach, something that freaks you out just that little bit.

And third: unwavering faith that Allah has heard your du'as and that your prayers have been set in motion the minute you uttered them.

Your Turn!

For this section, I want you to put into practice the art of making a sincere du'a, so use the McDu'a template to write down a du'a for your wildest dream.

1. Begin with *istighfar*.
2. Send peace and salutation on Prophet Muhammad/praise Allah.
3. Make a personal du'a using the ninety-nine names of Allah. Connect your dream du'a to your *deen*. If you don't know what to say, begin with the questions you first set out to answer in part 1:
   1. Who are you?
   2. Where are you?
   3. What do you want?
   4. Why do you want it?
   5. How are you going to achieve it?

   Begin with Dear Allah, it's me... Go ahead, I promise you, our Maker will be overjoyed to hear from you! Tell the One where you are (e.g., I am lost, I am confused, I am in pain). Say what you want (e.g., I need your help) and why you want it (e.g., I want change, I want to make a difference, I want a meaningful life that will guarantee a seat in Paradise), and then ask Allah for divine guidance (e.g., How can I achieve my dream?)
4. Recite your favourite du'as from the Quran and Sunnah.
5. Send peace and salutations on Prophet Muhammad/praise Allah.
6. Have the firm belief that goodness is coming your way, and finish up with Prophet Yunus's du'a/say *ameen*.

The art of making du'a:

→ Believe, expect positive outcomes, know that your du'a will be answered. Allah never leaves us empty handed.

→ Be in a state of *wudhoo* and face the *qibla*.

→ Raise your hands.

→ Send salutations upon the Prophet and Praise Allah.

→ Make du'a for others and encourage them to do the same for you too.

→ Give charity/do a good deed/ random act of kindness.

→ Be grateful.

→ Repeat your du'as.

→ Ask from your heart.

→ Use the names of Allah, all ninety-nine. Find a name of Allah that corresponds to what you're asking for and then create your du'a based on that.

→ Make du'a in key moments. for example, when it rains, when travelling, when fasting, in *tahajjud, laylatul-qadr*.

Meet Queen Rania

An Awesome Queen

Queen Rania of Jordan is a powerful advocate for education.

Did you know...

➜ As the wife of the King of Jordan, Queen Rania uses her platform to improve the education system. She is known for empowering women both locally and globally and is the voice for innovative and quality education for children all around the world.

➜ Amongst her many achievements, Queen Rania has been celebrated for

- founding the Queen Rania Foundation for education and Development,
- receiving numerous awards for her work with UNICEF/UN,
- writing several books.

"If you educate a woman,
you educate a family."

CHAPTER ELEVEN

Pray Big to Play Big

When I reflect on my road to religiosity, I remember feeling over-whelmed and not knowing where to start. If this is your first time, you might be feeling slightly overwhelmed too. Especially now that you're done with designing your du'as and learning the art of du'a, you may be wondering how you're going to incorporate it into your daily life. I mean, you're busy enough as it is!

I feel you. There's a lot to take in, which is why this chapter is about showing you how I've managed to incorporate du'a into my daily life. Follow me as we find out

How can I make du'a a part of my life?

Now, I know what you're thinking... You've just let out a deep sigh after the last chapter and you're thinking, *Dude, that is way too much work. I don't have time for that! There is so much to do, so many du'as to recite. Where do I start?*

As I walked toward my path to piety, I felt the same. However, I came across a *hadith* where a Bedouin came up to Muhammad and said "The laws of Islam are burdensome for me. Tell me of something that I will be able to adhere to. He said: 'Always keep your tongue moist with the remembrance of Allah, the Mighty and Sublime'" (Ibnmajah:3793).

This story resonated with me deeply because, as a perfectionist trying to perfect my Islam, I had reduced my spirituality to a burdensome list of rules and regulations. They were often hard to keep up with because I was trying to do too much at one time. I feared that if I didn't do it all I would be in trouble with God.

As a child, my relationship with God was based mainly on fear as opposed to love. I imagined Allah as an undercover cop, hanging in the background just waiting to catch me out! This idea stayed with me well into my mid-twenties until I actively worked on diminishing those limiting beliefs.

I really don't blame myself for that way of thinking because at every turn I was reminded of the doom and gloom of death and hellfire by those around me. I was bombarded with what's *haram*, what I'm not

I want you to know that Islam isn't hard; we make it hard on ourselves.

allowed to do, who I'm not allowed to be. Practicing Islam didn't seem like a fun thing to do.

The only reason why we often feel disconnected from Islam and Allah is because we lose ourselves to the rules and regulation. We reduce Islam to a list of do's and don'ts and as a result we lose sight of the greatness of God.

In Arabic, the term *remembrance* is known as *dhikr*. Our faith increases when we make *dhikr* and decreases when we stop making *dhikr* in our daily lives. If we want to feel *barakah* and live a life that we love, our daily lives should revolve around du'a and *dhikr*.

Dhikr (remembrance of God) and du'a are not meant to be a set of rules and regulations; they were gifted to us so that they can become rewarding habits. Inviting the miracle of du'a into your life takes effort and practice until eventually it turns into a more effortless habit.

So, what will these habits look like for you on a daily basis? You can experiment until you've found the right rhythm, but in the meantime, I can offer you a snapshot of a day in the life of my du'as. There are days when I slip up and don't do it with as much gusto as I could. There are also days when I don't make du'a at all and that's okay— we're human, not angels. But on the days I do make the effort and do my best to be present and tuned in as I follow this routine, I know I'm setting myself up for an exceptional, extraordinary day.

Remember that there are many good ways to build an effective routine where du'a is a part of your everyday life, and it really is down to personal choice. Ultimately, you must do what works for you.

Most of my du'as are done in the morning because over the years I've worked hard at becoming an early bird. Research has shown that mornings carry a unique and powerful energy that I like to make the most of.

My morning routine

1. As soon as I open my eyes I say my morning du'a.
2. I pray *fajr*.
3. I stay on my mat and recite the *Fatima tasbih* (*SubhanAllah* 33 times, *Alhamdulilah* 33 times, *AllahuAkbar* 33 times, followed by *ashadulailah illah*.
4. I make du'a using my McDu'a template.
5. I recite a page of Quran or *Surah Yasin*.

My bedtime routine

1. I pray *isha*.
2. I stay on my mat and recite the *Fatima tasbih* (*SubhanAllah* 33 times, *Alhamdulilah* 33 times, *AllahuAkbar* 33 times).
3. I recite *Ayatul Kursi*.
4. I recite the last 2 verses of *Surah Baqarah*.
5. I recite *Surahs* 112-114.
6. I recite *Surah Mulk*.
7. I make du'a using my McDu'a template.
8. I ask for protection from the hellfire followed by the Shahadah.
9. I recite my bedtime du'a.

If you're thinking you don't have time for that, make time!! If you're looking at my long list and thinking you'll start tomorrow, bear in mind that a habit is something you do every day, not something you do only when you're in the mood.

If you're serious about achieving your ambitions, you need to focus on what you're doing right now. Not tomorrow. What you're doing today gives you a very clear vision of what you'll be doing tomorrow, next week, next month, or even next year.

Believing that your future self will somehow be more disciplined without doing any of the work to discipline yourself will simply never work! Unless you have some strong rituals and habits in place, all the things you're doing today aren't going to lead you to the future you envision for yourself.

Having said all that stern stuff, what I've shared with you is a list of habits that took me years to build. I want you to understand that even a small daily habit can have a major impact on your life if you stick with it long enough. Good habits should be something you want to maintain for the rest of your life.

If all this is too overwhelming, you can wean yourself into a routine. Start with one or two elements and gradually expand as your threshold gets stronger. And if even that seems unachievable, then make a playlist with the *surahs* and *adkhars* I've mentioned. You'll find loads of beautiful recitations on YouTube. There are tons of great apps that let you play offline as well, so play them first thing in the morning and last thing at night.

When I first began adding du'as to my daily life, I started with just a handful of short ones because I was afraid my attention span wouldn't be able to handle it. If you feel like you won't be able to handle it either, be gentle with yourself. Remember that Allah loves quality, not quantity.

It has taken me a long time to master my morning and night routines. It has not been easy as it requires consistency, especially on the days I don't feel like doing it. But research shows time and time again the power of routine is incredible. There are so many du'as that are applicable to however you're feeling throughout the day. Recite them often, make them a part of your daily routine, and watch the difference in your life.

I wish so bad that I'd memorised these life-changing du'as earlier, instead of memorising the lyrics to Mariah Carey songs. I genuinely feel the *barakah* and relief that comes from incorporating short and sweet du'as to all my situations, whether I'm in a good place or in dire straits.

When thinking about the theme of this book, perhaps the most inspiring du'a is Prophet Ibrahim's. Whenever you feel as though your dreams are far out of reach, always remember that the reason we Muslims stand tall facing the *kaaba* today is because we are a result of an audacious dream Prophet Ibrahim made thousands of years ago. He dreamt a dream about nations of Muslims worshipping the Oneness of Allah when at a time he was considered a nation by himself, when there were literally no Muslims but he.

As he built the *kaaba* with his own hands he made du'a that believers would gather in that place to worship Allah. And now, thousands of years later, we still gather in the same place to celebrate his profound du'a.

That you are reading these words right now is a sign that Allah wants you to pour your heart and soul out in du'a, bare your truth in all its glory, and ask Allah for what you truly want.

So go make d'ua.

I have no doubt that my life has only been as awesome as the du'as I have made over the years. Everything I've achieved, everything I experienced didn't cross my path randomly; it came to me because I was very intentional about the way I was making du'a for the things I wanted for my future, and then taking the often scary but necessary actions to turn those dreams into reality.

"

I've noticed
how things
fall into place
when I've used du'a
to guide me.

"

Sometimes we overlook the small things and just make du'a for the big things. Remember always that Allah only has to say 'Be' and it is. If you make a habit for asking for the little things, then naturally you will always turn to Allah first for the bigger things. Ask Allah for everything, even if it is just shoelaces.

> **The miracle is truly in the moment that we pray. If you want to change your life, change it with du'a.**

Your Turn!

Creating a routine is important because through it you create a life that you love. There are no wrong or right ways to create a routine; all you need to do is come up with something that works for you.

You might be an early bird like me, so the morning will be the time to spend your energy and focus reciting Quran, making du'a, and meditating. Or you might be a night owl, so carve out a routine that you could use for *tahajjud*. It doesn't have to be a lot, but it does have to be consistent.

What *surahs* will you recite?

What *dhikr* will you recite

What *du'as* will you recite?

Meet Khadija bin Khuwaylid

An Extraordinary Entrepreneur

Khadija was from Saudi Arabia. She was a remarkable leader in business and commerce in a male-dominated society.

Did you know...

- Khadija is lovingly known as the "mother of the believers" and was the first love, first wife, and first woman to embrace Islam.
- Khadija was a very successful businesswoman in her time. She used her intelligence, confidence, and business acumen to create a thriving business and then spent most of the profits to help the poor.
- Khadija is an inspiration to all the widows as well as single mums out there as she was widowed twice before she married Prophet Muhammad.
- Khadija was a strong, independent woman.
- She challenged stereotypes by proposing to a man fifteen years younger than she and was a leading businesswoman at a time when women had very few rights and baby girls were being buried alive.

"I was the first ever Muslimah."

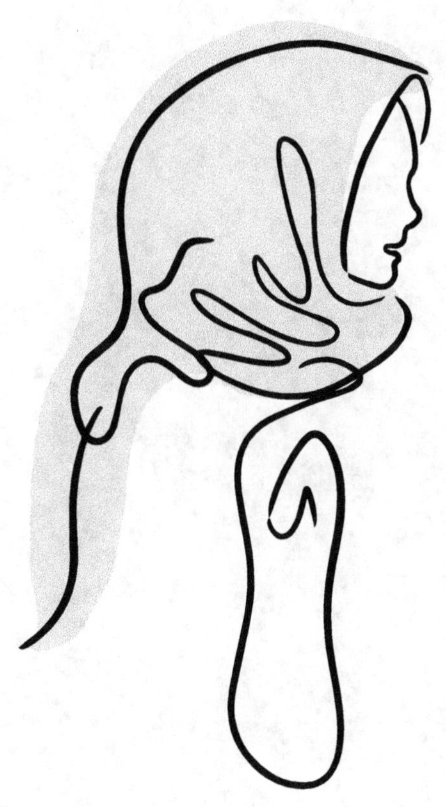

STEP 3:

do

CHAPTER TWELVE

The Power of Visualisation

You made it to step three! Think of this as the producing stage. This is the bit where it really gets fun. I'll be sharing some of the best tips and techniques I've learned over the years to manifest my wildest dreams, and you get to put everything you've learned about dreaming and du'aing into practice!

You may find the upcoming chapters very instructional (or even slightly bossy!). Consider them your personal to-do lists to check off as you go along. Unlike the previous two parts of this book, each chapter stands alone, but when combined they create a powerful roadmap to a destination where your wildest dreams are waiting for you.

For those of you who have dared to dream and relied on the power of du'a to see it through, I see you, sista, and I salute you! Come with me on this last leg of our adventure as we find out

What is the first thing big dreamers need to do?

If you want to live a life that you love, the first thing you need to do is imagine yourself living it. You'd think that's common sense, right? But it isn't always common practice. Not everyone can let their imagination run free. I know this because I hear it from women around me all the time.

I can't begin to tell you how many times friends and family have said 'You lucky cow!! Your life is one big holiday! I wish I had your life!!' after they've seen my Snapchat posts by the pool in the sun or canoeing with my kids.

And it drives me bonkers!

Not because I get hurled all sorts of colourful verbal abuse, but because they think that my life is only achievable for me and totally unachievable for them. It's so frustrating to hear the women I love stopping themselves before they've even started because they're wishing for the same things I have, but they are not *imagining* those things for themselves.

And so I ask, when you're thinking about the lives of women you admire, are you doing the same thing?

If you are, here's what I want you to know: If you can't imagine yourself living that life or achieving that goal, then guess what. You won't!!

Sometimes we do imagine a lofty future for ourselves but then we sabotage it by comparing ourselves to those who are doing better than we are. It's easy to get so discouraged we stop ourselves right bang in the middle of our tracks because the head finds it impossible to imagine what's in the heart.

Sometimes we become fixated on waiting for that one big calling to come knocking on our door, and we end up never pursuing anything because our ideas don't seem big enough, hashtag-worthy enough, or earth-shattering enough.

Many moons ago, when I first dreamt of becoming a teacher, I said to my husband, "You know, babe, after I graduate, first I'm going to get a job in that college near our house then I'm going to apply to work at colleges in a Muslim country so we can go live there."

I suspect by then he was so used to me daydreaming out loud he switched off as soon as I opened my mouth to speak, leaving me to wave my arms around like a madwoman, deliriously talking on and on while my wishful words went in one of his ears and out the other.

Yes. I was daydreaming again. I couldn't help it. I liked to carry big lofty dreams in my back pocket. I liked to imagine the impossible. But guess what happened because of me dreaming big? In due time I became qualified as a teacher and I got both jobs!

Coincidence? No. I was simply practicing the art of visualisation.

At that moment of my life, I may have just enrolled in a course to qualify me as a teacher, I may have had just one kid as opposed to *kids*, but I saw my life not as it was, but as it could be.

Now I can guess what you're thinking: You're rolling your eyes and thinking that dreaming of becoming a teacher isn't exactly the biggest, most outrageous dream, is it? In fact, it's quite an ordinary one, boring even.

But for me, for that season in my life when I was juggling the bitter-sweet chaos that comes with being married young, turning up on time to my part-time job despite coping with a nocturnal teething baby, becoming a teacher was my version of shooting for the stars.

I saw myself working as a lecturer in the college near my house. I imagined what it would feel like skipping to nursery with my baby boy on the way to work. I imagined standing on top of my classroom table, like Robin Williams in *Dead Poets Society*, as I inspired impressionable young minds to look at things not as they were but as they could be, and it excited me!

In due time, this is exactly what happened (apart from the *Dead Poets Society* re-enactment scene, of course, because no one in their right mind wants to get sued for vandalising college property).

I continued to visualise a high-flying career in education somewhere roughly around the Middle East, while real life was going on around me. A few years later we had just had our daughter and I was out of work. We were so bloody broke we couldn't even afford to pack our bags for a holiday, let alone afford to pack our lives to relive our immigrant parents' past in a fancy foreign country.

But I got excited imagining the possibilities!

I got excited at the thought of not having to wait an entire year before my family could holiday by the beach. I literally got goosebumps as I thought about hearing the *adhaan* live and uninterrupted five times a day, or when I pictured my kids growing up knowing that there was so much more to the Islamic calendar than just the holy month of Ramadan.

And I would no longer be required to waste God knows how long reading the ingredients section on the back of my biscuit packets to make sure it was halal (#secular world shopping problems).

When I dreamt those dreams there was no way of knowing if they would ever become reality, but almost everything I envisioned has come true one way or another.

For instance, right now as I type this sentence, I am indeed basking in the glorious sun and watching my kids play by the beach. (Relax, *haram* police, you can quit gasping. I'm sunbathing with my oversized sun hat and my burkini on! Zero skin on display!) Now, I'm not saying that your aspiration has to be the same as mine or that in order to achieve your big dream you need to uproot everything and move to the nearest Sharia-compliant continent.

What I am saying is that if you're dreaming of becoming a change-maker, like Tawakkol Karman, you need to be able to see yourself owning that stage and inspiring others. If your ambition is to become an astronaut, like Nora Al Matrooshi, you need to be able to visualise yourself in that spacesuit floating off to Mars. If your goal is to become a model, like Mariah Idrissi, you better start practicing that pout right now.

Whatever your dream, you need to be able to see it with the utmost clarity in your mind. That's why visualisation is so important: If you can see it in your head, you can hold it in your hand. Fact.

The mind thinks best in images, so the concept of visualising is a powerful way to get into a manifesting mentality. If you're not crystal clear on what you want your life to look and feel like, then I'm afraid it's just not going to happen. Another fact.

Visualisation can come in many shapes or forms. It could be thoughts in the shower or it could be through journaling where you intentionally write down exactly what your visions are. It could be through intentional meditation where you close your eyes and imagine what your life would be like once you achieve your goals. It could be through thinking through your plans with your friends.

There is no right or wrong way to create a vision board, so use whatever floats your creative boat. Whatever your method, the idea is that you focus your mind, get real clear about your goals, and let Allah do the rest. I'm going to take you through how I go about my personal favourite: the vision board.

Now before you skip the rest of the chapter because you think I'm about to ask you to get out your craft scissors and colouring pens, I want you to know that it's not the type of vision board you're probably imagining.

Although it must be a lot of fun, I don't the patience to cut out pictures from magazines, draw cute doodles, and stamp out quotes on a board the size of my window. Instead, what I want you to have a go at is creating a vision board using one my favourite apps: Pinterest.

How to make a vision board

For this task, I will ask you to bring only three things: du'as, images, and the audacity to dream big. The idea is that by the end of this activity you'll have a whole list of personal du'as at your disposal that you can look at and make du'a wherever and whenever you want. Over the years this digital vision board has done wonders for me, and I'm sure it will do the same for you too.

When creating your vision board, remember this: There is no dream too big or too small for Allah to make into reality. There is so much we could ask Allah for, and as you know from part 1, Allah is waiting for us to ask.

Our beloved Messenger told us to "Ask Allah for all your needs even if the strap of your sandals break" (Tirmidhi:3604i).

So, how do you start making this awesome vision board? Rather than a Pinterest page of random pictures and fancy quotes, I want you to imagine your vision board as a holy version of Google maps.

What you're about to create is an intricate map that will lead you all the way to J-town (that's *Jannah*, in case you're wondering!). First, you'll need a picture of the place we all want to end up. Obviously, there are no pictures of Paradise on Pinterest, so what you could do is find an *ayah* or a quote that mentions it.

Next, you need to figure out your starting point, which is where you are now, and look at the steps you need to take to get to your ultimate goal, then pin out the different places you're going to go to get there. This is where all your big and small dreams come in. Find a picture or a post to match each dream and pin it to your Pinterest board.

When you set yourself a long-term goal, you focus on your destination. When you set yourself short-term goals, you break your map into smaller, walkable steps.

Remember your SMART du'as? Add them to your vision board too. Adding your du'as to the vision board is powerful because not only are you seeing what you want, the writing prompts you to at least read it, if you're not saying it aloud. There are editing features on Pinterest that let you title your board, organise your images, and write notes on your posts, so use that space to write down your du'as.

Now, I'm not guaranteeing that by creating a vision board you'll miraculously manifest everything you've ever wanted, but I can guarantee that it is an excellent way to keep you motivated and work-ing toward your goal. Every time you utter the du'a written on your board, you walk one step closer to your dream.

You'll also need to put a giant asterisk on the side of your board because death (or a deadly pandemic) can strike at any time. I don't mean to pop the balloons on your parade here, but whether we like it or not, whether we are fully practicing Islam or not, death will come and even the biggest dreamers need to be mindful of this reality.

In *Surah Al-Anfal* (8:30) we are reminded of the fact that "Allah is the best of all planners".

Don't feel bad when your dreams don't move according to your plans. If something goes your way, say *alhamdulillah* because it has gone according to your plans, but if something works out a different way, say *alhamdulillah* again because this is what Allah has planned for you.

Remember, it is perfectly okay to not achieve your dream first time or even second time round. I had a dream to drive, but it wasn't until I took my driving test for the *fourth* time that I passed!

A vision is the most powerful thing we as humans can have; it gives us a sense of purpose. Be stubborn about your visions, but at the same time be flexible with your methods. If at first you didn't succeed, try, try, and try again, because as cheesy as this sounds, success is not a destination, it's a journey.

Your Turn!

Create a vision board of all your dreams by writing them down as du'as.

For example: Instead of writing "travel to fifty different countries before I turn fifty", write "Ya Razzaq, give me the *rizq* to travel to fifty different countries before I turn fifty".

Remember to connect your du'as to your goals in *dunya* as well as the *akhira*.

Meet Ginella Massa
A Remarkable Reporter

Ginella Massa is a Canadian news reporter who hosts her own show.

Did you know...

→ Ginella made history by becoming the first ever *hijab*-wearing journalist to appear on national TV and is currently hosting her own show, *Canada Tonight with Ginella Massa.*

→ Ginella has over a decade of experience in news reporting, whether it's been locally or nationally on air or behind-the-scenes, in television or on the radio.

"Don't let anyone else silence your dreams because of their perception of what you can or cannot achieve."

CHAPTER THIRTEEN

Pray on Time, Every Time

When I was younger, my relationship with *salah* started and ended with my basic five-a-day, if that. It took me years to unpack the fact that praying was never about Allah; it was ultimately and always for me.

Nowadays, I'm the first to preach that creating a strong routine around mindful prayers is fundamental to achieving your wildest dreams, not just in this life but for the afterlife too, and my biggest regret is ignoring this truth for such a long time.

In this chapter, walk with me as I walk you through why I think it's so important to create that routine and to pray on time, every time. We'll take a deep look at how this (often mundane) act of worship is so powerful, so grab yourself a pair of funky binoculars as we zoom in on the number one secret to success and ask ourselves

How does the quality of *salah* impact the quality of our success?

Every day, we are invited to pray through the sweet, melodious sound of the *adhaan*. Some of us are invited through one of those *adhaan* radios, some of us through an app on our phone, and others through their local *masjid*'s loudspeaker. I used to rely on Islam Channel.

Wherever we may be, when the *adhaan* is heard, we get to decide whether we should continue doing whatever we are currently doing, or rise and accept the call to success. In *Surah Al Mu'minun* (23:1) Allah tells us that "successful indeed are the believers". From this verse, we learn that praying is the prerequisite of our success because as a believer, our day begins and ends with the *salah*.

When the *adhaan* is called, the Arabic words we hear are "*haiya 'alas-salah, haiya 'alal-falah*". This literally means *come to prayer come to success*. The fact that these words were specifically chosen to invite us to our prayers shows just how deeply our potential, our productivity, and even our prosperity is dependent upon this beautiful act of worship.

Salah is an obligation on every single Muslim to pray five times a day because we have been commanded to do so in the Quran and the Sunnah. It is the next most important pillar of Islam, after the *shahadah* (testimony of faith). The reason we pray is simple: to show humility and utter submission to our Creator, all day, every day.

Praying doesn't just help us remember our Creator, it also creates discipline. It reminds us that *salah* isn't an option; it is the minimum standard required of every Muslim and is a ritual that requires us to stand up and bow down on time, every time.

Think of the *fajr, dhuhr, asr, mughrib*, and *isha* prayers as specific reminders scattered throughout the day to let you know that it's boot-camp time. They are there to discipline you, to train you, to whistle in your ears, and to push you to become the best version of yourself.

They are there to teach you to stand, bow down, prostrate, and sit in humility each time, every time; they are there to teach you to repeat the same tasks over and over again until your brain creates those important neural pathways to make those life-changing habits; but most importantly they are there to inspire you to keep going. Especially on the days when you feel like you can't.

In both *Surah Ta'ha* (20:14) and *Surah Al Ankabut* (29:45), Allah reminds us to "establish prayer". I used to oversimplify this *ayah* and think that we're being told to just pray. However, what Allah is telling us is that to ensure that we are successful in our ventures, we need to institutionalise *salah* into our daily lives.

The way we prioritise our daily prayers mirrors our level of discipline and determination for our other big goals. Only when we have a systematic approach toward *salah*, when it is anchored deep in our hearts as well as our homes, can we see the results of its ripple effect everywhere else.

> **_Salah_ does to our soul what exercise does to our body. It strengthens us.**

Salah teaches us consistency.

It totally makes me cringe to admit this, but my childhood friends would be the first to tell you that the most annoying thing about me when I was a kid was that I used to be flaky AF. I would organise coffee dates and cancel on my girls last minute. I would set deadlines only to never meet them. I would make promises of fasting, dieting, or keeping secrets only to break them shortly afterward.

At the slightest complication, I would flop on my plans to meet someone or do something, and to make it worse, I could never be honest about why. Instead, I would lie that a heinously unforeseen circumstance meant I had to bail on my commitments last minute.

Oh yes! I was flaky as a fruit pie.

Looking back, it's totally obvious why I lacked such integrity and discipline. I mean, how could I possibly keep my commitment to anyone else when I couldn't keep the most basic commitments to not

We can't just show up for the famous five when we feel like it.

just God, but also myself? Every prayer I missed created a neurological pattern of flakiness until it became an effortless habit and rippled out into all other aspects of my life.

I didn't realise it at the time, but the cure to my inconsistency was to keep persevering through the fog, to pray especially on the days I didn't feel like it. When we internalise the fact that *salah* is not a choice and become consistent in our prayers, we learn to turn up, day in day out, for everything else as well, whether we like it or not.

It wasn't until late into my twenties that I got into the rhythm of keeping promises to myself. I was a mother of two by then, I was done with my flakiness, and I wanted to show up, if not for anyone else then at least for my children.

In staying dedicated to keeping even my most basic commitments, I eventually began to trust myself. This had a massive impact because not only did it give me the confidence to rely on myself, it also meant that I honoured my commitments to other people. *Salah* taught me to become consistent.

Salah provides structure and stability.

As I write this book, we're witnessing a pandemic so apocalyptic that I feel like we're filming for a scene straight out of *Contagion*. No doubt one of the biggest challenges we've all felt during the pandemic is our loss of structure due to the disruption of our daily routines. And because we no longer had the usual scaffolding to give our days a sense of purpose, life could feel pretty chaotic.

It got to the point that I was no longer putting eyeliner on and getting ready to go to work. Instead, I'd be wearing my neatly styled *hijab* over crumpled pyjamas as I conducted meetings online at my kitchen counter.

I had no idea what day of the week it was because it felt like one long weekend. I'd forgotten what it feels like to get on a plane, or even drive out of town for dinner with friends. I couldn't remember the last time I saw my family in the flesh, and my kids? Well, there was only one word to describe them: feral.

Life as we know it, has changed.

However, the one thing that helped me navigate my new normal was the routine that my prayers had already created for me. My day revolved around my *salah* and not the other way round.

By nature, most of us are creatures of habits. I certainly am. We love rules and routines because they structure our day and provide the stability we need. Research also shows that routine is instrumental for mental health, and so praying at specifically assigned times is exactly the medicine we need to flourish.

However, despite knowing this, many of us go through life feeling slightly under-flourished. We are constantly drowning in distractions. Popular culture teaches us to sedate ourselves anytime we feel pangs of anxiety, melancholy, or fear by binge-watching TV, by drowning out the voices in our heads with the songs on the radio, by endlessly scrolling through our phones or online shopping on our laptops. We have access to these weapons of mass distraction.

Think of all the silly mistakes we make at work, at home, or even in our relationships. Think of all the typos that appear in our texts, posts, or emails. Think of all the irrational decisions we make, simply because we aren't capable of being present enough.

The cost of becoming so easily distracted is destructive, because when faced with diffi-cult situations we rarely think before we speak or act. Being distracted makes us more likely to be reactive rather than proactive. But when we master mindfulness, we summon the power to choose our battles wisely and inevitably have much greater control over our actions.

Salah is our superpower. It calms our mind and controls our thoughts so we can concentrate on what really matters. When we approach our ambitions with clarity, we become indestructible.

To reach this level of indestructibility, we need to enter a space of heightened awareness: tranquillity as well as humility. In Arabic this is known as *khushoo*. In English, I believe the word on the street is *mindfulness*. Either way, it teaches us to become present, to become mindful of our inner voice, and it strengthens our intuition and ability to focus.

In a noisy world, *salah* allows us to be silent. The word *silent* is a perfect anagram for another: *listen*. Praying is that quiet simple ritual that allows us to switch off so we can listen to our heart, to our mind, to our body, to our soul, to become centred and whole again. And when we are quiet, we can also hear what God is trying to say to us.

However, as Muslimahs, practicing mindfulness is more than just sitting with our eyes shut tight and taking deep breaths in and out as we listen to a soundtrack of waves crashing onto a shore. Practicing *khushoo* means to not just practice awareness of ourselves but to also submit wholeheartedly to the awareness of love, fear, and awe of Allah.

Khushoo is so powerful because it begins in our hearts, transforms our minds, and then its effects are manifested through everything we do. This is how we create a life that we love.

To become a *kashi'een* means to become someone who has mastered control over their wandering heart and mind. When you are in a state of *khushoo*, you pray with full concentration and pay attention to the meaning of the words you are reciting. Your heart is fully present on the prayer you are performing, and your mind and body are fully present to the greatness and glory of God.

Research shows that practicing mindfulness not only can impact our mood but also impact the world around us. What we could do with such laser-focused attitude and action is staggering, and I for one, am waiting with bated breath to see what you will do with yours!

So how can we become more present in our prayers, realistically and easily?

It would be a lie if I told you that I pray all five of my prayers with perfect *khushoo*, because as much as I would love to, I'm not there yet.

I do, however, make an intentional effort to practice being truly present in my prayers every day. I do this by choosing a specific time of the day when I know that I am least distracted. For me, this is before *isha* time, the last *salah* before we go to bed. This is the perfect time for me because my monsters have gone to bed, I've clocked out of work, and I'm done with my chores. I dedicate the last hour before I sleep to myself.

We hear so much about self-love these days, but sometimes self-love can come in the form of sitting on your prayer mat, taking time to quietly contemplate and recite the Quran.

We are invited to practice mindfulness five times a day.

Khushoo is the practice of intentionally turning your attention away from distracting thoughts toward a single point of reference. When I am trying to practice *khushoo*, I just focus on my breathing as I try to imagine the *kaaba* in front of me. I take long, deep breaths and notice them moving up and down my body, and when I feel distracted by thoughts, I simply draw my attention back to the present moment until eventually I am ready to stand in *salah*.

Giving myself those precious moments to relax and realign my intentions before I start praying does wonders for my spirituality. When done with *khushoo*, I always leave my prayer mat renewed and rejuvenated. It is especially in those moments, when I have taken the time and effort to get into the zone, that I taste the sweetness of *salah*. After I've finished praying, I recite a collection of *adkhars* using my *tasbih* and follow up with some recitation of the Quran. Sometimes I focus on one of the ninety-nine attributes of Allah and repeat the name over and over as I try to focus on its meaning.

Sitting in the solitude of prayer even for five minutes is not easy, but persevere. Start with five minutes before or after your prayers, then gradually increase the time as you build your spiritual muscles. If done regularly, you will find that practicing *khushoo* will become easier and more enjoyable and you will begin to value your prayer mat for what it truly is—your sacred space.

If you have read chapter 11 from step 2, you'll know that another favourite time of mine to practice my *khushoo* is as soon as I wake up. I find that it is usually easier to be present during the early hours before my mind has had a chance to start whirring! Even non-Muslims in the coaching and self-development industry rave about the powers of waking up before sunrise, a precious time of the day, which we know as *fajr*.

Research suggests that your brain is like a sponge when you wake up: It will absorb whatever you feed it. You may feel tempted to reach for your phone to check messages, news feeds, or the weather. But this is the best time to recite, reflect, and reconnect with your purpose.

As you walk along this path to meet the greatest version of you, have the startling belief that these five daily steps were prescribed so you can experience greatness beyond your wildest imagination. As Muslims, we know that this is the first act of worship we will be questioned about when we are buried six feet under. So use this powerful ritual to work for you, in this world and the next.

We are invited
to success five time a day,
the question you have to ask
is will you accept
the invitation?

Your Turn!

Create an action plan for one or two times during the day where you can actively practice *khushoo* in your *salah*. There are many simple changes we can make to improve our *khushoo*, which in turn will improve our relationship with our *salah*. Here are a few tips to get you started:

1. **Be mindful as you take the steps to wash yourself in *wudhoo*.**
   Start with *bismillah* and focus on each action of the *wudhoo*. As Muslims, we are taught to pray as if it's the last time. Imagine if this was the last time you will be making *wudhoo*; how much time and effort will you take on it?

2. **Be aware of *salah* timings.**
   There are great apps to help you do this. The one I use is Athan, which calibrates the *qibla* and the *athan* for me wherever I am in the world.

3. **Be prepared for prayers.**
   You can do this by setting an alarm on your phone a few minutes before the *adhaan*, laying out your prayer mat, sitting somewhere quiet, and disengaging from whatever you were occupied by. Sitting at least five minutes before it's time to pray helps silence your mind and concentrate on being present.

4. **Be conscious.**
   Salah is not a two-minute task to be checked off your to-do list. It is a conversation between you and your Maker, so make every effort to understand what you are saying. Make the effort

to understand why you are reciting each *surah* and what lessons they are teaching you. When you make a conscious effort to study the *salah*, you will find that you are more present in your prayer.

5. **Be confident that Allah is watching you.**

   Most of the time we forget that Allah is watching us and waiting to grant us what we wish for. When we rush through our prayers, we are sending signals to our brain that this is something unimportant and therefore doesn't require our focus or attention.

6. **Be consistent.**

   Make a list of a few *dhikrs* and du'as that are easy on the tongue and research which *surahs* are beneficial to reflect on during each specific prayer, and recite them consistently for every prayer.

Salah is our saviour.

It is our certainty in an uncertain world. Whether we are happy or sad, rich or poor, healthy or sick, winning or dusting ourselves off to try again, *salah* is an anchor in our lives. If you're serious about making your dreams a reality, you need to pray on time, every time.

Make a pledge to yourself today to take full responsibility of your *salah*. Don't use past or present circumstances as an excuse not to stand before your Maker, and rise.

Khushoo checklist

- Did I do my *wudhoo* properly?
- Did I pray on time?
- Do I know the meaning of the words I recited?
- Did I focus on the movements of each *salah*?

Create a routine for *fajr/dhuhr/mughrib/asr/isha*

My example: *isha*
- → Recite *istighfar*
- → Recite evening *adkhars*
- → Make du'a
- → Recite *Surah Mulk*

> **When you change the way you show up for *salah*, you change the way you show up for your dreams.**

fajr

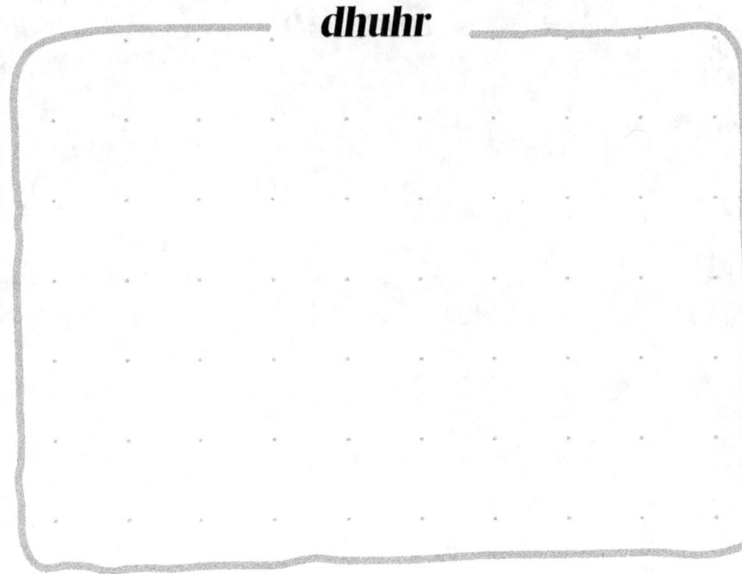

dhuhr

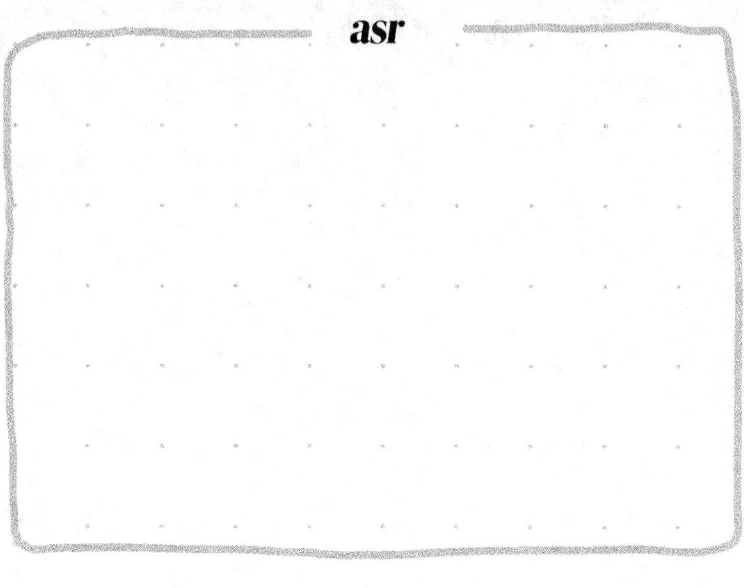
asr

mughrib

isha

isha

Meet Mariam Al Ijliyyah

An Ace Astronomer

Mariam is Syrian and is known as the only female astronomer in ancient Islam.

Did you know...

→ In the tenth century, long before compasses, GPS systems, or clocks were invented, a brilliant scientist who became known as Mariam al Astrulabi invented an astralobe, which is an ancient calculating device.

→ Because Muslims must worship Allah facing the *qibla* no matter where we are in the world, Mariam's invention helped locate the position of the sun, moon, and the stars which were used to find not only the *qibla*, but also to find out the times of prayer and what days Ramadan and Eid could be celebrated.

"Because of my incredible dream you get to use apps to show which way the *qibla* is whenever you want to pray or use a sat nav whenever you are lost on the road!"

CHAPTER FOURTEEN

Embrace an Attitude of Gratitude

In this chapter we will explore what it means to make the conscious decision to focus on blessings instead of the bad, every single day. We will also get to meet Lady Luck's evil stepsister, Lady Lack, and get to understand why she's not someone we want to hang out with.

The key takeaway from this chapter is that just as we get to choose success five times a day, we also get to choose gratitude at least five times a day. The ride ahead may get a little bumpy at times as we question if we are truly thankful for all our blessings, but it will all be worth it as we learn

What's the connection between being wildly grateful and my wildest dreams?

When I first moved to the UAE, an interesting habit that I noticed amongst my new non-Muslim friends was their use of the word *alhamdulillah*. It was refreshing to see them express gratitude with a word I was so familiar with, yet in a tone that was foreign to me.

Their faces would literally beam as they gave thanks and praise to God.

How was your weekend? *Alhamdulillah!*

How are you feeling? *Alhamdulillah!*

How's chemotherapy going? *Alhamdulillah!*

Up until then, I was used to hearing it as a half-hearted, monotone expression; it was basically our British way of telling each other that we were keeping calm and carrying on.

For most of my twenties, grounding myself in gratitude was not something that came naturally to me. In fact, I struggled with it, which is why many of my dreams failed to come to life.

Every day I'd stand in front of my mirror and fight with my feelings of ingratitude and decide which aspect of my life it would dictate that day. My litany of lack was endless: I wasn't pretty enough, I wasn't perfect enough, I wasn't petite enough, and the one that would make me feel the worst of all, I wasn't pious enough.

And just like that, I spent most of my twenties with my BFF, Lady Lack, by my side. We had some great girls' nights in, face masks on, eating ice cream straight from the tub, thoroughly relishing the feeling of never having enough and never feeling good enough.

Gratitude is an attitude that I learned to cultivate over time. I wish I had adopted it much earlier, which is why I desperately want you to know about it today.

Up until recently, gratitude wasn't studied as a phenomenon because it seemed like a simple human emotion. However, researchers are now beginning to unpack the effects of gratitude and have discovered a magical truth that when you give thanks, you receive more to be thankful about.

Of course, now that I'm in my thirties and as I have gotten better at becoming more *Muslamic*, it doesn't surprise me that research is now confirming what religion has been telling us all along—that gratitude is good for us.

In *Surah Ibrahim* (14:7), Allah Almighty says "If you give thanks, I will certainly grant you more". What I love about this verse is that it doesn't say exactly what you will receive more of, but Allah says just enough to give hope that the possibilities are limitless. This verse also reminds me about the power of the law of attraction: that what you send out to the world is what comes back to you. In Islam we don't have karma, but we have *kifara*. We are taught that what we give is what we will get back. We are taught that we can be magnets of goodness, and the more we show that we are grateful, the more we will attract things to be grateful for in and around us.

The secret then, is that when it comes to achieving success in any of your endeavours, you need to be in a space where you have both unwavering faith in your du'a being answered by Allah and unfaltering gratitude for what you're about to receive.

Research studies on happiness suggest that grateful people report higher levels of positive outcomes psychologically, emotionally, and physically. Happy people enjoy better health, better relationships, and richer social interactions. They are less likely to be anxious, stressed, or depressed and more likely to be successful at work, more prosper-ous, productive, and creative, and as a result enjoy living a life that they love.

However, though being in a state of constant appreciation is good for us, it's not always easy. A big part of why I lacked a more graceful approach toward gratitude is because I was so busy obsessing over

Good things come to those who are grateful.

all the things I didn't have, I simply forgot to be grateful for all the things I did have.

Everything I had was because I made du'a for it at one point. That job I complained about, that baby who kept me awake all night, that apartment I lived in... I should have been humbled by all those blessings but somewhere along the way, I forgot. I forgot that every blessing I had was just that, a blessing.

In the Quran, Allah often uses the word *insan* to describe we human beings. In Arabic the root of this word means *forgetfulness*, which shows that because of our tendency to be a bit scatter-brained, we assume that we're entitled to everything we have. We take things for granted and often get bored of our blessings because we simply get used to them.

Through this verse I came to know that like every other act of worship, I wasn't doing God any favours by being thankful; rather, this was God's favour on me. See, Allah is not affected by my gratitude or ingratitude because Allah is Al Ghani, the Self-Sufficient. Expressing thankfulness doesn't benefit Allah in any way; ultimately it benefits me.

Here's what you should know: Gratitude is more than just a bunch of empty platitudes. You don't get to recite your *alhamdulillahs* a hundred times on your *tasbih* after *salah* and be done. By now you and I know enough about the brain to know that it can sense when we are being insincere, and so can God. Being grateful isn't one of things you can fake.

So how can you keep it real? In *Surah An Naml* (27:19), Prophet Suleiman recited a very useful du'a to help him embrace an attitude of gratitude:

Through Prophet Sulaiman's du'a, Allah teaches us two great ways of embracing an attitude of gratitude:

1. Seeking inspiration to be grateful.
2. Seeking ways to express that gratitude.

Lesson 1:

Seeking inspiration

to be grateful

There are many examples in the Quran and *Sunnah* where we are taught how to seek inspiration. In *Surah Al Furqan* (25:62), Allah reminds us that the only way to nurture gratitude is through meaningful contemplation and reflection, by looking at our surroundings and becoming more mindful of the blessings we take for granted.

We are taught that to truly adopt an attitude of gratitude, we must strive to be amongst "those who remember Allah while standing, sitting, and lying on their sides and reflect on the creation of the heavens". In this *surah*, we learn about a beautiful du'a.

Rabbana ma Khalaqa hatha batila subhanaka faqina adhaban- naar. (Our Lord! You have not created this in vain. Glory to you! Save us, then from the chastisement of the fire.) *Surah Ali' Imran* (3:191)

When we take a minute to pause and breathe in the beauty of the world around us, we can't help but be filled with gratitude for the truth that there is no God but God. Even if our mouths can't find the words to express this gratitude, our hearts can't help but utter this truth.

Another practical way of living in a constant state of awareness that we are the recipients of all kinds of goodness is by keeping a journal to log the things you are grateful for. Now before you sigh and decide you don't have time for it, let me convince you why it works.

Having an attitude of gratitude is a bit like having a shower. You can't just shower once and expect to smell like your shower gel for the rest of your life. Similarly, if you want to stay thankful you're going to have to motivate yourself to be grateful every single day, especially on the days when you don't feel at all grateful.

Research shows that just two consecutive weeks of daily gratitude practice can boost your level of optimism and mood, and that can last up to six whole months! And that's not all. Those who kept gratitude journals on a weekly basis were reported to generally feel better about their life compared with those who moaned about their life.

For me, the best time to record my gratitude is in the morning. I usually record things I'm thankful on an app called happyfeed, which asks me to note down three things I am grateful for every day. I always write two things and leave the final box blank; this inspires my mind to be on the lookout throughout the rest of the day.

This simple practice of journaling joy can be life changing. When I started to do this daily and created those important neural pathways to establishing it as a habit, it didn't take long to realise that when I made a habit of appreciating the smallest things, bigger and better things to be grateful about kept coming my way.

Lesson 2: Seeking ways to express that gratitude

The second part of Prophet Sulaiman's du'a teaches us to express gratitude by doing righteous deeds. When we receive a gift, it's not enough for us to feel good, we have to do good. We must do something in return, which creates a wonderful cycle of receiving and giving, giving and receiving.

When we are grateful to God, our human instinct tells us to pay the kindness back. Now, since Allah is limitless and free from ever wanting or needing anything from us, obviously we can't pay Allah back for all the wonderful things we've been given, but we can pay it forward.

Paying it forward doesn't have to be money or grand gestures. It could be something as simple as posting a kind compliment online, opening a door for someone, picking up litter, making someone feel good when they are around you, or even giving someone a smile. In an authentic *hadith*, our beloved Messenger tells us

"**Your smiling in the face of your brother is charity, commanding good and forbidding evil is charity, your giving directions to a man lost in the land is charity for you. Your seeing for a man with bad sight is charity for you, your removal of a rock, a thorn or a bone from the road is charity for you. Your pouring what remains from your bucket into the bucket of your brother is charity for you**" (Tirmidhi:1956).

When we allow ourselves to give or do wonderful things without expecting anything in return, those random acts of kindness transcend into abundance and put us in a position of more abundance.

However, when we're too scared to share and worry that there won't be enough to go round, guess who's likely to make a guest appearance in your life again? Yep, that's right, my good old friend Lady Lack.

Whatever it is that you send out to the world, that's what you will receive from Allah. Allah's Messenger said

Although giving charity is an important part of our faith, giving generously is not always easy. Most of us have a slightly screwed relationship with money because no matter what language our parents spoke, we grew up hearing that money doesn't grow on trees, that there isn't enough to go round.

In Arabic, the word for sustenance is *rizq*. The moment we truly appreciate that our *rizq* has already been written for us, we will no longer feel the need to hoard our money, recipes, ideas, knowledge, feelings, or anything else.

Maintain a mindset that prosperity is coming your way. Say *bismillah* when you tip the waiter or pay your bills. Say *alhamdulillah* when you pay your *zakat* for another year. Give lavishly, whether it is with your time, money, or energy because through this outrageous act of sharing you will receive more *ajr*, more blessings than you could ever imagine!

In Arabic, *alhamdulillah* is such a beautiful, all-encompassing word because it means that we are thanking and praising Allah simultaneously. This is the true essence of gratitude. Thankfulness comes in the form of acknowledging the goodness you witness in your life, and praising is understanding that you had no claim on the gift or benefit you received; it was freely bestowed out of compassion, generosity, or love.

Experiencing the grace of gratitude needs to be consciously cultivated every single day. The reason it is Sunnah to recite a du'a beginning with *alhamdulillah* as soon as we wake up or begin our prayers with *Surah Al Fatiha* is so we have an attitude of gratitude from the minute we open our eyes to the minute we close them.

Looking at gratitude through this lens makes us humbly recognise that we could not be who we are or where we are in life without our Creator. We begin to understand that our health, our wealth, and everything between is a gift from God. We begin to understand that the only way to truly thank God is not just by saying we are grateful but showing we are grateful through doing good.

Our dreams are the most precious gifts from Al Wahab, the Giver of Gifts. What we do with that gift is not only our gift back to the world but also our biggest show of gratitude to God.

Your Turn!

There are so many ways to be grateful! My favourite method is writing a list. But if whipping out a notebook and writing 'Dear Diary' is not your cup of tea, remember that there is no wrong or right way to record your gratitude.

Whatever your method, make a habit of recording what you're grateful for consistently. When you are genuinely appreciative of everything and everyone around you, your brain begins straight away to give you reasons to believe that more is possible and more is to come.

In the following section, use Prophet Sulaiman's strategy to embrace an attitude of gratitude. **Rabbi awziAAnee an ashkura niAAmataka allateeanAAamta AAalayya waAAala walidayya waan aAAmala salihantardahu** (27:19). (Lord, inspire me to be thankful for the blessings You have granted me and my parents, and to do good deeds that please You).

1. Seek inspiration to be grateful (what are you grateful for?).
2. Seek ways to express that gratitude (how can you show you are grateful?)

For the first part, brainstorm all the different things you are grateful for. It doesn't always have to be noble; it could be anything ordinary.

For the second part, think of different ways to express that gratitude, how you can pay it forward. If you're stuck, here are some ideas.

→ Recite a du'a. There are many du'as from the Quran and Sunnah that help us express our gratitude. Make a habit of memorising them.

→ Give your time and attention to someone you are grateful for. Let them know that you appreciate them.

→ Pick a couple of charitable causes that resonate with you and commit to giving money every month. It doesn't have to be a lot, just consistent.

→ Share your knowledge! When you teach what you know to others, you get to learn it twice.

→ Find a cause or project to support by volunteering in your local community or online.

What are you
grateful for

grateful

Meet Zainab Al-Eqawi

A super scuba diver

Zainab is an Iraqi pharmacist, para-athlete and television presenter.

Did you know...

↪ Zainab lost her leg at the age of seven when a bomb went off in her home in Iraq during the Gulf Qar. However that didn't hold her back from achieving her dreams. As well as scuba diving, she keeps herself very busy.

↪ She is an advocate for the rights of disabled people especially in the Middle East.

↪ She's worked as a television host for *Yalla Banat*.

↪ In July 202,1 she graced the cover of *Vogue Arabia*.

↪ In 2021, she was named as a regional face of The Body Shop's Global Self-Love Movement campaign.

"Life doesn't stop when you have a disability."

CHAPTER FIFTEEN

Love the Skin You're In

Self-love is a journey in itself! It's a bit like going on a trip with only the North Star as your guide; you might never arrive but at least you can say you were going the right way!

This chapter is dedicated to what is meant by self-love and why it is important as we go about chasing our wildest dreams. Hang on to your *hijabs*, girls. This is going to be a rollercoaster of a chapter as we finally find the answer to a question once asked by Tina Turner:

What's (self) love got to do with it?

I've recently started dance classes. (Oh chillaaax, *haram* cops! I go dancing in a strictly woman-only gym and we groove to clean music, okay?) I do salsa on Saturdays, belly dancing on Tuesdays, and any other classes I can squeeze in. You should know that this story isn't about how I used my newly acquired knowledge of positive psychology and neuroscience to become a dancing queen. No, this story is about a fabulous dancer in my class who always stops me in my tracks mid-shimmy as I take a moment to admire her.

But this story isn't about her groovy moves either. It is a tale about how she dresses up for every single class.

Let me make it clear that we aren't preparing to get four yeses on *Arabs's Got Talent*; we're just getting a weekly workout in a gym tucked away in a little corner in Abu Dhabi.

But for salsa, this woman comes in with a halter top, a swinging skirt, and four-inch heels. For belly dance she has her harem pants with one of those hip scarfs with dangling coins. For street dance she comes in with a baseball cap fashionably sideways on her head, bright trainers, matching leggings, and a sweater tied casually round her waist. And just last week I got to class a bit early and found her practicing ballet in a pink tutu and real ballet shoes!

I mean, what a legend!

Someday I hope we can be mates. But for now, I admire her from a distance. I want to tell you what I have learned from her.

I have learned that how we look on the outside dramatically impacts how we feel on the inside. I have learned that we need to turn up for our passion, unquestionably looking every inch the part. I have learned that whether we want to become a dancer, a doctor, a police officer, or even a local lollipop lady, we absolutely need to look the part.

I have also learned that she leaves the studio covered head to toe in traditional Islamic attire. And so she also reminds me very poignantly that in order to show up for our faith, we need to dress the part for that too.

As my religion became more and more a part of my identity, it became never enough to just say I was a Muslim. I felt the need to act like a Muslim by eating like a Muslim, acting like a Muslim, talking like a Muslim, and, importantly, looking like a Muslim, which is the ultimate declaration of love for my faith.

However, I realise that this opinion of mine can be contentious.

I have been amongst too many practicing sisters who think that being devout means looking drab and dreary. That we should patiently wait until we enter *Jannah* to rock our designer frocks because it doesn't matter what we look like on the outside, it's the inside that counts, right?

I shake my head and disagree.

I have also seen practicing sisters who really don't see how the way we dress can affect us spiritually. They feel it's not necessary to cover our head, shoulders, knees (*and toes! Knees and toes!*) because again, Allah judges what we look like on the inside, not the outside.

I disagree here too.

In psychology, researchers found that we don't just think with our brain, we also think with our body. The clothes we wear not only have the power to impact our mood, they can also impact a whole host of other areas, including our attitudes and behaviours, our confidence, and even the way we interact with others. This is known as enclothed cognition. My dancer friend obviously knows this, which is why she rocks up to my dance classes the way she does.

Now, I'm no expert on the *fiqh* of fashion, but I reckon if we really wanted to investigate what a Muslimah looks like at her most authentic, it would probably resemble something very close to what she looks like when she prays.

As a Millennial who grew up in the shadow of Islamophobia and in the glare of the incandescent light of feminism, I am well aware of the complexities of looking like a Muslim in non-Muslim countries. Looking visibly Muslim can be a tough choice to make.

In a world where there is already so much debate about how much or how little we should wear, it is important to realise that my opinion or yours does not determine how we dress. Because as we know from

Surah an Nur (24:31) and *Surah al Ahzab* (33:59), our dress code is a commandment, not a choice, and Allah who is Al Musawwir, the Fashioner, would never command us to do anything unless it is good for us.

Sis, our faith doesn't teach us to cover up because we are ashamed of our body; it teaches us to cover up because we are proud. In an authentic *hadith* we learn that Allah is beautiful and Allah loves beauty. Allah wants us to look our most beautiful inside and out. Allah wants us to dress well and take pride in our appearance because Allah knows that when we look good, we feel good.

Throughout history, women of high status in many cultures and eras have dressed beautifully and modestly. It is for this reason that you will never see pictures of the Queen of England wearing tight, skimpy dresses or Mother Teresa in a hot pink leotard and why portraits of the most respected woman in Islam, the Virgin Mary, or Mariam as

> **Remember that our non-Muslim friends don't read the Quran or *hadith*—they read us.**

we know her, are depicted in a way that demands nothing but respect and reverence.

Dear sisters who sit on both sides of the fence, I hear you when you say it's the inner beauty that counts, but what we wear on the outside matters. Without sounding too much like the blue lady from *Avatar*, the point I'm trying to make is that everything is connected, how we show up for anything reveals how we show up for everything.

Style and spirituality come hand in hand. Regardless of our fashion sense, we are all ambassadors of Islam.

It took me a very long time to really love the skin I'm in.

Ever since childhood, I have felt unworthy and ugly in a hundred different ways, but after years of unpacking my insecurities, I finally arrived at the truth: If I didn't love myself first, no one else could either. That if I didn't respect myself enough to know that I didn't deserve unkind words or abusive behaviour, no one else would either. That when it came to my dreams, if I didn't believe in myself, of course no one else would, and if I didn't teach myself about self-love, who would?

Although self-love is a trend tossed around as often as pancakes nowadays, it wasn't something I was familiar with growing up. Maybe it was called by a different name back then and I missed the memo, but it wasn't in any of the Islamic books I read, it wasn't taught by my parents or my school, and it certainly wasn't discussed in any of the conversations I had.

I realise now that self-love is everything when it comes to living a life you love. It is one of the most important conversations you can have with yourself because it impacts virtually every major decision you make.

Self-love can mean different things for different people because there are so many ways of loving the skin you're in, but to me, self-love is more than just having a good skincare routine or taking myself out on a date. To me, self-love means honouring and respecting the body I'm in.

The reason I bring my definition of self-love to your attention is because it breaks my heart to see beautiful Muslimahs who have let their relationship with their body distract them from their dreams.

It seems like our bodies are often just not getting the love they deserve.

Some of us neglect ourselves because we have other bodies to take care of. Some of us think our body isn't as important as our ambitions. Some of us are too busy comparing our body to someone else's, but the one that saddens me the most is when I see some misuse their body in the name of love.

Sis, forgive me for being a little candid here, but it's time we talked about another thing we never really talk about because it's still taboo. Your body is a gift from God, you know that, right?

Loving the skin you're in also means honouring and respecting your body enough to never feel pressurised to give the most vulnerable part of yourself away or expose parts of your precious body to any Ali, Abdul, or Mo who bats an eyelid at you.

In Arabic, the word for something borrowed is *amanah.* Your body is an *amanah* from God. It is a gift that needs to be treated with the highest respect because it will be eventually returned to its rightful owner.

Allah has chosen your body specifically to house your soul, and it is your responsibility to love your body because not only is taking care of it an act of worship, but also, as its earthly custodian, you will be held accountable for it.

So many Muslimahs struggle with this idea and spend a lot of their lives waiting for validation, if not from a man, then from others. If you're looking for that special someone to come and tell you that you're worthy enough, know that she is looking right back and winking at you from the mirror!

The problem is that we don't give ourselves the permission to love ourselves. Somewhere, we began confusing self-love with being selfish and we shamed ourselves into thinking our bodies don't deserve love because that would be narcissistic.

As Muslims, one of the first things we are taught is that Allah is Ar Rahman, the Most Merciful. We know that if we show mercy to those on Earth then the One who is in the heavens will show mercy to us; therefore, being kind and forgiving is an important element of our faith.

However, we often forget that mercy starts from within. After all, how can we show mercy to others if we can't be merciful to ourselves? How can we give to others if we can't give to ourselves? And how can we be truly kind to others if we struggle to be kind to ourselves?

Self-love means being confident, courageous, and comfortable in your own skin. It also means feeling totally okay with being perfectly imperfect. Your relationship with your faith, your aspirations, and with other people can only be transformed when you transform the relationship with the most important person in your life: you.

So breathe, and love the skin you're in.

Love yourself enough to realise that you deserve much more and then respect yourself enough to work hard for more.

Your Turn!

Self-love is a lifelong process and something that ideally needs to be nurtured every day. Once you have cultivated the skill of self-loving, it won't take long for you to see its effects seeping into all other areas of your life.

In the following section, make a list of all the ways you practice self-love. If you find yourself stuck, here's a couple of ways I try to be kinder to myself: First, I treat myself to the spa at least once a month. Second, I've become much nicer in the way I talk to myself; I am now more likely to forgive myself when I mess up and I avoid negative self-talk. Third, I am more aware of what I consume, whether it's through social media, TV, or music because I am aware that it impacts my thoughts, and I am more conscious about the food I bless my body with. And finally, I prioritise myself. This was the hardest to do because for the longest time I thought I wasn't allowed to put my own feelings or needs first.

Use this space to brainstorm all the different ways you can be kinder to yourself.

Meet Halima Aden

A Sassy Supermodel

Halima is American Somali and is the first *hijab*-wearing supermodel.

Did you know...

→ Halima was the first Muslim woman to grace the cover of *Vogue* magazine wearing the most visible marker of a Muslim woman's faith, the *hijab*.

→ Originally a refugee from Somalia, Halima became a UNICEF ambassador and used the strength of her story to advocate for refugee rights and human rights, particularly for children around the world.

→ Rather than seeing herself as a supermodel, Halima sees herself as a role model and understands the impact she can make on Muslim representation in the fashion industry.

→ Halima uses her platform to work with companies that best represent her and her faith.

"Don't change yourself, change the game."

CHAPTER SIXTEEN

Get Your Grit On

Not all journeys are easy. Some can be a real slog and some can leave you with a sore bum from sitting down too long! This chapter is about getting you moving; it's about understanding which behaviours and attitudes you need to adopt when you're out there chasing your crazy dreams. It's about appreciating the value of working hard as well as staying persistent, even when the road gets a little rough.

Get your work boots on as we dig deep to discover

What is grit?

You're a clever bird.

You know that when it comes to achieving your goals, being grateful, being mindful, being growth minded and confident aren't the only things you need to become Wonder Woman. Living your best life still requires something more.

Belief is good. Dreaming is grand. Du'a is great. But if you really want to fast track to awesomeness, what you need is grit. Heaps of it. And no, before you ask, I'm not talking about a certain type of porridge.

Grit—keeping going when it gets tough—is instrumental for achieving your wildest dreams. It is why some Muslimahs succeed whereas others fail. Grit is having the stamina to stick to your goals day in and day out. It's about enduring life like an episode of *Downton Abbey*, only this time you can't skip the bits that get boring or hard to watch.

For me, the ultimate OG of grit is Hajar, wife of Prophet Ibrahim, mother of Prophet Ismael, the founder of the holiest place in Islam, Makkah. Because of Hajar's miraculous discovery of *zam zam* water in the dry and barren land of Arabia, civilizations were able to build a city where billions of visitors still drink from the well even thousands of years later.

Hajar inspires me because when she was left in the middle of the desert with no food, water, or even shelter, she didn't break down in tears, become paralysed by fear, or feel sorry for herself. Nor did she sit around patiently and passively waiting for a man to rescue her.

Instead, she actively did something about her situation.

Even though she didn't quite understand why she'd been left in the middle of nowhere, she understood that her husband was following God's orders, so she trusted the process. Worried for the safety of her child, she began to run up and down two hills to search for passing caravans, searching for someone who could provide her with the aid she desperately needed.

And just to set the scene for you here, she wasn't running around in an air-conditioned building with cool marble flooring underfoot. She was running on hot desert sand under a blistering sun and with a wailing baby.

As the story goes, she climbed up to the top of Safa, looked around to find something... anything... but she found nothing so she ran to the opposite end to Marwa, to do the same, only to return with nothing more than a broken heart.

At this point, many of us in her position would give up and accept defeat. If there were CCTV cameras around in those days or she was in a reality TV show, we would have expected her to put her hands up in the air and shout "I'm a celebrity, get me out of here!" Instead, Hajar chose to have *tawaakul*. She chose to place her trust in Allah and actively pursue her goal even if it seemed impossible. And so she ran. Not once, not twice, but seven times!

Seven *freakin'* times in the blazing heat!

Seven long stretches of struggling to seek sustenance for her precious baby. Seven intervals of pushing herself past the limits of her worry and weariness. When she had done everything she possibly could, God sent the Angel Jibrael down from the seventh heaven to release the gushing miracle we know today as *zam zam*.

Hajar never gave up hope and she never lost heart. I can't begin to comprehend what it would feel like to walk in her footsteps, let alone run. It seriously hurts my head trying to understand the kind of hope and grit she must have had to just not give up.

Her goal to beat the odds and survive became a tribute known as the *sa'i* (to strive or to pursue something), an important ritual that millions of we Muslims perform as we walk the greatest journey of a lifetime—*hajj*.

What. A. Queen.

Hajar's story represents what it means to never become a victim of circumstances and accept failure as an option. In Arabic, the word for patience is *sabr*. This is a deeply active concept, not a passive one. *Sabr* requires us to be persistent and to persevere through our problems.

So, in *Surah Baqarah* (2:155) when Allah talks about testing our patience, it doesn't mean we sit patiently and do nothing. It means we rise up and rise to the challenge, as Hajar did.

Hajar taught me to be a warrior not a worrier.

In popular culture, we're programmed to think that if something requires hard work, it's just not worth it. After all, why waste your time when there's always a quick hack or shortcut available on YouTube!

We're so quick to quit projects, quit relationships, and quit trying the minute it gets a bit hard. We're constantly looking for instant gratification, quick results. We get discouraged easily and therefore quit on our dreams the minute it gets a bit uncomfortable.

In many cases, we have been seduced to the idea that being gritty is only relevant when it comes to sticking to our grand audacious goals. You may feel you don't have the guts to be gritty just yet and so you can't stick to achieving even your smaller goals. But being gritty in smaller goals is super important because small wins often lead to medium wins that inevitably cascade into big wins.

Having grit doesn't necessarily mean that winners never quit. It means that when you do find yourself trapped between a rock and a hard place, you find the passion and perseverance to do something about it.

So, how do we develop grit? Allah answers this question for us in *Surah Baqarah* (2:153) by telling us to "seek help through patience and prayer".

I love this *ayah* because it reminds me that if I'm serious about achieving my wildest dreams, I need to be in it for the marathon, not the sprint, which is why we are given patience and prayer as tools to help us through the slog. It took twenty-three years for the Quran to be perfected, which teaches us that great things take grit.

Sometimes we look at accomplished Muslimahs and assume they must have had it so easy, but that is far from the truth. What we fail to see beyond those pretty pictures, awards, and accolades are women who achieved their wildest dreams through sheer grit.

We look at Fatima's life, Jamilla's body, Sarah's business, or Amara's relationship and we let their success talk us out of chasing our own dreams. But what we don't see behind their swag is their sweat. We see happiness, not hard work; we see success, not sleepless nights. What we don't see is grit.

Every great writer, illustrator, designer, inventor, researcher, or leader will tell you that every dream they accomplished began with just an idea, but what brought the idea to life was their commitment to work on it until they ended up with a masterpiece for the world to marvel at. It didn't happen accidentally; it happened with a spoonful of sugar and a lot of grit.

If there's anything I've learned about dreaming big and failing first time, second time, or even third time round is that failure is how we acquire grit. It's about being willing to stick to something no matter how long it takes.

Grit can look like different things to different people.

For me, grit looks likes being committed in a fun and loving marriage for over fifteen years despite going through rough patches where I've loved my man more than I've liked him. Grit looks like gritting my teeth as I gave birth to our kids and persevered through the exhaustion of staying up all night taking care of them.

For me, grit looks like walking for miles and miles in the baking heat during *hajj* and having to hold back my tears and my breath simultaneously while using the notorious squat bogs at the end of a gruelling day.

For me, grit looks like trying to make a life in a new country when I didn't know how to speak the language, how to find a place to live, how to make new friends, or even how to drive on the other side of the road, all whilst holding down a full-time job, entertaining constant visitors from England, completing my master's degree, and raising my babies.

For me, grit is why you are holding this book, reading my story, and (I hope) coming to the realisation that if I can walk through this process of not feeling expert enough, experienced enough, or holy enough to produce a project as terrifyingly epic as this, you can too.

Grit is perseverance.

> **Grit is being completely terrified by what you're about to do and going for it anyway.**

Perseverance is praying on time, every time, waking up for *tahajjud,*
reciting *Surah Mulk* every night, reciting *Surah Yasin* every morning,
reciting *Surah Khaf* every Friday even when you feel emotionally far
away from God.

It's about fasting even though your stomach is grumbling and growl-
ing at you. It's about stuttering over words as you try to understand
verses from the Quran even though Arabic isn't your first language.

Perseverance is working daily on your inner critic to let go of limiting
habits and beliefs, showing up in the gym, showing up for your job,
showing up for your family, but mostly showing up for your goals,
especially on the days you don't feel like it.

If you're staying up late to watch an episode of *Friends* instead of
working on that project, or just daydreaming about getting a promotion instead of making sincere du'a about it, then know that you've
got grit wrong. When you find yourself struggling and have no passion
left to persevere, push yourself to keep persisting and remind yourself
that if Hajar can do it, so can you.

Girl, go get your grit on.

Your Turn!

Use the following section to think about how you are practicing grit.

Now, you may be thinking *Wow, that's all great, but I just don't think I can be as gritty as you*, let me stop you right there. Yes, you can.

How many jobs have you hated but you showed up on time every morning? How many years of school did you go through even though you felt like it was a complete waste of time?

How you grow your grit is down to you. You can wake up for *tahajjud*, you can fast twice a week, you can set a target of reading a certain number of books, you can take up jiu jitsu at your local gym. Whatever it is, know that you don't have to be born with grit, it can be cultivated. It's all about guts and perseverance.

In the following space, make a list of things you want to get done and commit to finishing at least once a day, week, or month. Stay persistent and single-minded in the pursuit of achieving your goal.

Knowing that you can't give up will force you to overcome challenges and prove to yourself that your abilities are not fixed. They can be developed with the power of grit.

What is grit?

Write down what grit looks like for you.

Here are some examples of how I get my grit on:

Daily

- ☐ recite at least one page of the Quran
- ☐
- ☐

Weekly

- ☐ go to the gym at least twice
- ☐
- ☐

Monthly

- ☐ finish reading at least 3 books
- ☐
- ☐

Short-term goals

Long-term goals

Meet Ibtihaj Muhammad

An Awesome Athlete

Ibtihaj is an American sabre fencer who was the first American woman to compete in the Olympics in *hijab*.

Did you know...

- Ibtihaj was not only the first ever American to compete at the Olympics in a *hijab* but the first Muslim American woman to walk away with a medal.
- As well as being a five-time World medallist and World Champion, she is also an activist shattering stereotypes for Muslim women.
- She is also a fashion designer and launched a modest fashion label, Louella, as well as helping Nike develop the Pro Hijab. Ibtihaj even has her own Barbie, complete with sabre, fencing mask, and *hijab*.

"We are all born with something that God has given us and we owe it to ourselves to discover what that gift is, and to change our families, our communities, and the world. I truly believe our purpose is to leave a positive mark on the world."

CHAPTER SEVENTEEN

Find Your Tribe

In this chapter we will travel back to me telling you more about my local gym. Don't worry, I won't bore you with more descriptions of the dancer I'm stalking... This time I'll tell you what I've learned about friendships from my Zumba classes.

We will discuss why friendships can make us or break us on our journey toward dreaming big. You may have to open a couple of tabs in your head as we browse what happens when we "go compare" our lives or our dreams with our friends.

We will be taking some awkward turns here, so you may want to hold tight.

Brace yourself as we go in full speed to answer

What does the company I keep reflect on me?

Back to my dance classes. I don't know what she eats for breakfast, but my Zumba instructor is just as luminous as the neon tank tops she rocks up to the studio wearing.

What I absolutely love about my Zumba classes is how the teacher brings an entourage with her every week. Yep! That's right, a freakin' entourage! I mean, *who does that*? And guess what? They're just as fun and fluorescent as she is. They randomly break into dances mid merengue march and grab you by the arm to take you along for the ride. What a hoot!

What inspires me most about these classes is that this tribe of hers come down to the gym purely to support her, to make sure that her classes are the best that anyone has ever been to, and I've got to admit, they really are the best I've ever been to.

If you ever happen to pass by my neck of the woods, please feel free to pop your head into one of our classes because what you'll see are women of all shapes and sizes hilariously happy, ecstatically getting their steps wrong, but who cares because we're having so much fun whistling and hollering and cheering each other on. This gig goes down every Monday at five p.m.

I have to say, I've learned a few cool moves but what I've learned most of all is how important it is to surround yourself with some ride-or-die cheerleaders who'll always have your back, no matter what. Living your best life can get a bit lonely if you don't have others to share it with.

Tons of research suggests that people are at their happiest when they can share their dreams with deep meaningful relationships, and one of those powerful relationships can be found in true sisterhood.

Your friends are a bunch of crazies you've decided to share this adventure called life with. They are the shoulders you lean on when you need a good cry and the backs you smack when you're laughing so hard your belly hurts. They are the misfits who help you figure out how you fit into this world.

I have been blessed with many beautiful friendships and I am so grateful that my girls have stuck around to encourage me to dream big, especially on the days when I felt so little.

I've heard that we end up resembling the five people we spend the most time with. The company we keep defines us more than we know and reveals who or what we are and what we truly worship.

Our lovely Prophet said "Man follows his friend's religion, you should be careful who you take for friends"(Riyadussalihin:367).

This *hadith* teaches us that we need to be very intentional about the company we keep because, whether we admit it or not, our circle of friends can have a huge influence on how we feel, think, and even behave.

In another *hadith*, our Prophet also said

"A true believer is a mirror of his brother" (Adab:238).

We naturally mirror the thoughts and behaviours and even the personalities of those we spend the most time with. You might scream and cover your face when your best friend's finger gets squashed by the car door; you find yourself yawning just because the person next to you is yawning; or you may start smiling for no reason other than the fact that you caught one of your besties cracking up. Neuroscience explains this with the concept of "mirror neurons"; psychology calls it social contagion.

In *Surah Az Zukhruf* (43:67), Allah reminds us about the final hour, when "friends, on that day, will become enemies to one another, except the God-fearing". This verse teaches us the importance of keeping good company, because friends won't just benefit us in this life but also in the afterlife.

If you want to live an extraordinary life, you need to intentionally seek friendships that grow you and keep you moving forward, even if you feel like you have plenty of friends already.

Finding your tribe and surrounding yourself with big dreamers who will wholeheartedly support you isn't always easy. If you don't have them in real life, then find them online. The World Wide Web is full of inspiring and enthusiastic Muslimahs who can't wait to root for you!

As you mature, you will discover that good friends and time are two of the most valuable things to possess. Finding the right friends is so important because if you're surrounded by a posse of pessimists who are constantly finding lame excuses for not living a rewarding life, chances are you'll be doing the same.

With time, you may also begin to realise that some of your friendships are based on convenience and are not entirely helping you cultivate the skills and mindset you need to achieve your wildest dreams.

You probably are friends because you've grown up in the same neighbourhood or went to school together, but if your friends aren't inspiring you to become the best version of yourself, staying BFFs for the sake of a shared history won't help either of you.

Another reason it's important to have the right calibre of friends around you is that just as it is easy to copy each other, it's even easier to compare ourselves with each other.

We all know that the comparing culture is bad for us and yet we low-key almost enjoy doing it. We look at Amal's body, Mya's new kitchen, Sarah's business, or Asma's kids and we let their failures or accomplishments make us feel good or bad about ourselves.

From a very young age, we've been conditioned to compare ourselves with our siblings at home, with our friends at school, and when we grew up, with our colleagues at work. I'm pretty sure we'll still be comparing ourselves with each other even when we've lost all our teeth and are wobbling around in our Zimmer frames.

Using each other as reference points has been common practice because it has been the most useful way to not only learn from one another but also to gauge whether we are falling far behind or missing out.

Comparing ourselves with our friends lets us do two things. First, it minimises our doubts about certain aspects of our lives. For example, *Am I doing this parenting thing right? Better check what Ameera feeds her kids for dinner.*

Once we catch up with our bestie and find out what she feeds her children, the information from the conversation allows us the chance to define ourselves. For example, *What? Ameera's kid is using a spoon to feed herself at nine months old and self-soothes herself to sleep every night at six p.m?*

Ugh. I must be a bad mum.

Whether it's comparing our handbags, holidays, houses, or hashtag-worthy date nights with our husbands, we like to compare ourselves with each other as a way of measuring our own growth. Comparison is how we tell if we're making progress.

Having awesome high-flyers around us sounds great in theory because they can motivate us to improve ourselves. However, comparisons often bring out the competitive or self-critical streak in us, and when it gets out of hand it can eat away at the confidence of even the most self-assured Muslimah, especially now that social media allows us to see how we measure up to not just friends that we know in real life, but also friends that we've added online.

Because of our lifestyles and the new normal caused by the pandemic, we keep up with a lot of our friends online. Our fascination with constantly checking each other's carefully curated posts and obsession with celeb culture has exacerbated our tendency to compare ourselves with each other in real time, all the time.

This makes us vulnerable to endless exposures of perfect people in perfect images, living perfect lives, but it also makes us vulnerable to the point that we second-guess our worthiness.

When we compare ourselves with friends who are doing far better than we are, we may ooh and ahh and give them high-fives to let them know we're proud of them, but as genuinely happy as we are for them, some of us can't help but pit their present success against the shame we feel for a future failure we haven't even attempted yet.

What happens next is that we let their highlight reels make us feel low. We don't even give ourselves the chance to show up for our dreams because when we look at another Muslimah who has already been there, done that, we decide that we're never going to be as perfect as they are, and so, sadly, we never even try.

We use our sisters' successes as a reason to not even try, deciding that we are no way near as creative, as beautiful, or as talented as *she*.

Then of course we shame ourselves for feeling the shame.

Now, I'm not going to pull up statistics to show you that comparison is one of the main reasons so many women feel depressed, have anxiety attacks, or even have suicidal thoughts. I won't sit here and lecture you to let go of competing and comparing either, because I know you'll carry on doing it anyway. We're wired to do it. But what I will share is how I made this toxic habit work for me, instead of against me.

Research tells me that when it comes to the comparison game, we tend to compare ourselves either upward or downward.

In upward comparisons, we generally compare ourselves with the friends that we believe are doing better than we are in one way or another, in the hope that they'll inspire us to be more like them. In downward comparisons, we look at people who we feel are worse off than we are, in the hope that will make us feel better about our own crappy life.

> **Comparison is a killer. Especially now, when we have the power to compare everything and everyone from the palm of our hand.**

In Islam, we are taught that everything serves its purpose best when it is done in moderation. Too much upward comparison can cause us to become insecure or jealous, whereas too much downward comparison can cause us to become arrogant and boastful.

In an authentic *hadith* we learn that our dear Prophet said

> **"When one of you looks at one who stands at a higher level than you in regard to wealth and physical structure he should also see one who stands at a lower level than you in regard to these things (in which he stands) at a higher level (as compared to him)"**
> **(Muslim:2963a).**

Through this *hadith* we are taught that when we look up at those we admire, it almost feels like we are beneath them, inadequate even. We feel like we have less in comparison, which inevitably makes us feel the good old FOMO.

But when we look at those who are less fortunate, the opposite effect happens; all of a sudden we begin to feel as though we have more and as a result we feel more grateful for the blessings we already have.

The way I see it is that it doesn't make a difference whether the glass is always half full or half empty, because in the end it's a simple matter of how you feel. If you feel like you have a lot, you're happy, but if you feel like you don't have a lot, you're inevitably unhappy. The reason we're all so obsessed with comparing is because, deep down, we just want to feel good about ourselves, to have the confirmation that all the madness we feel or think is somehow normal.

Look, I'm not going to pretend that it's all unicorns and sunshine out there. I've had to lose some mates in my lifetime, but I've also gained some terrific new ones. Girl power and all that jazz makes a great foundation for great friendships, but that could all be ruined in a single moment if we don't channel our energy to compare in the right way, which brings me to another by-product of comparing.

One of the ways in which the comparison game can spiral out of control is through our inability to control our innate nature to be jealous.

Jealousy is the sharp pang in the pit of your stomach when you see your friend with something that you want. You feel it when she tells you that she just got engaged, you feel it when you hear that she just got the keys to her new house, or you feel it when you see that she just got a promotion at work and is now earning a much higher salary than you.

Even though we know jealousy is an emotion that good Muslim girls shouldn't feel, we feel it anyway. And when we try our best to suppress that feeling, our body betrays us by feeling negative energy toward the person we're jealous of.

This negativity is then manifested in different ways. We may feel annoyed or angry when we're around her; we may end up gossiping about her, avoiding her, being cautious around her; we may suddenly become fake, passive aggressive, or hostile toward her; and if we're a complete nutjob, we may blank her just for fun.

I want you to know that this is all normal. We are normal.

Believe it or not, this is simply your brain protecting you. When you compare yourself to someone else, your brain knows that you

But what if jealousy can be good for you?

can't handle all those complicated feelings so it replaces them with something easier to deal with, such as annoyance or anger.

Jealousy gets a bad rap even though it's totally normal to feel that emotion. We all feel it at times, and chances are, the more we look for success, the more we'll find to compare ourselves with.

We often suppress those feelings of jealousy and avoid admitting how we feel even to our closest sisters. We act fake and pretend that everything is okay because we think it's wrong to carry the burden of comparing and competing.

In that moment when she shares good news with you, but you feel nothing but pangs of jealousy, ask yourself why you're feeling this way. What is her success saying about you? Where do you feel that you're lacking?

What if that weird, anxious, hostile, and uncomfortable feeling toward your friend having something that you want is simply your body telling you to take action? To achieve your goals just as she has done.

I'm not encouraging jealousy, but if you feel this way (and you will feel this way at some point) why not use it to your advantage? Jealousy can be a signal, giving you information on what you want for your life, on what your values are. Why not listen to that voice in your head and do the work to discover more about the areas of your life you might need to pay attention to?

If you see your mate thriving, whether it be spiritually, financially, physically, mentally, or in any other way, the bravest way to overcome jealousy is by asking her for genuine help. From personal experience, I can guarantee you that if she is a real friend, she'll be more than happy to share her secrets.

She'll tell you about her own anxieties about her self-worth, she'll tell you about her struggles with her husband or her faith or her business, and she'll be more than happy to share her tips for success with you. A true friend wants you to win just as much as she is winning.

We rarely like to admit that we are jealous of each other. But having those brave conversations would not only deepen your friendship, it would also normalise something we spend so much effort subduing. Being honest and asking for help gives you the opportunity to strengthen your friendship and also gives you the chance to see the reality of what you perceive to be perfect.

Once you hear what it took for her to achieve that qualification, relationship, accolade, or figure, you'll realise that you only thought you wanted what she had, because if you were to be given the same blessing, you might not want it after all.

For instance, you may think you want her flat stomach, but once you learn that she fasts religiously every Monday and Thursday and does two hundred push-ups every day, you may think twice. You may want to be a blogger like she is so you can get all those freebies, but once you learn that she stays up half the night editing her videos after she puts her young twins to bed, you may decide that your sleep is far more important. It goes back to that *ayah* in *Surah Baqarah* (2:216) where Allah says *"Perhaps you would hate a thing while it is good for you; and perhaps you would like something that is bad for you—Allah knows, and you know not".*

Compete against the *same old lamo* you were last year. Be worried that five years from now, your *eman* is in exactly the same place. Be so engrossed in your own goals that you don't have time to compare other people's highlight reels with your blooper of a beginning.

In Arabic, envy is known as *hasad*. It's different than jealousy. When we talk about *hasad* in Islam, it isn't just about looking at your best mate and wishing you had the same as her (jealousy); envy is looking at that friend who has more than you and wishing that her blessings be taken away from her regardless of whether you have what she has or not.

Being on the receiving end of envy is not fun. It can even make you sincerely doubt yourself and question whether your dreams are realistic. In numerous *hadiths*, we are advised to "Seek refuge with Allah, for the evil eye is real" (Ibnmajah:3508) and "If there was anything that could overcome the Decree then the (evil) eye would overcome it" (Tirmidhi:2062). Both these *hadiths* teach us that the destructive nature of envy affects us more than we think, which is why we are encouraged to recite *Ayatul Qursi* and *Surah Falaq* before we go to sleep every night. And yet we invite *hasad* into our lives anyway.

We live in a culture where we feel obliged to announce things that have or haven't even happened yet. And unless you're amongst the small percentage of sociopaths who enjoy sharing good news to intentionally make others feel bad, most of you would want to share your blessings with others for innocent reasons. But the truth is, not everyone wants to hear or see that you're doing well.

You may find this discomfort expressed in a variety of ways: people make funny faces when you mention your dream, or say mean things to tease you whenever you talk about it. They may block you on social media, exclude you from certain things, or if they're really desperate, they may resort to downright wailing on the floor, grabbing you by the ankles to do whatever it takes to stop you from going after your dream!

"Mina, are you sure you want to quit your secure nursing career to open up a bakery when you've got four kids, a mortgage, and rheumatoid arthritis? What if you fail?" Or in my case "Are you sure you want to drag the kids halfway across the world? What if you go there and can't cope!" Might sound like they've got your back and mean well, but the root of their fear is that your big dreams remind them of what they lack.

When you share something that makes your friend feel awkward or insecure, the point of sharing your good news is lost. Just as you might react negatively toward someone else's positive news, not everyone is going to be over the moon for you.

If your friend is having problems conceiving, your proud baby bump can be painful to see, or if she's going through a heart-breaking divorce, whether she wants to or not she may feel a pang when she sees the flowers your husband just gave you.

Some sisters are not as privileged as you, and as much as they have the same potential and desire to achieve their dreams, due to their background they can't achieve those dreams quite as easily. Sometimes people are so self-unaware they don't even realise that they're projecting *hasad* onto you.

There is a time and place for sharing. Being mindful of people's struggles and being selective with what you share and with whom can be a powerful way to avoid the *evil eye*.

Your Turn

We all have that one friend who's always thinking that everyone's eyes are out to give her the evils, right? You know who I'm talking about. Her car breaking down, her nail polish chipping off, or her cat dying are all consequences of *hasad*. Oh, and that's why she didn't do well on her business page on Etsy.

Don't be that girl.

In this section, make a plan to help you stay on track whether you feel jealous or are on the receiving end of someone else's jealousy. Research and write down du'as you can recite if you're feeling envious or feel the effects of envy.

If you find yourself becoming paranoid because you feel someone is jealous of you, here are a couple of tips:

- **Ask for protection.** Seek refuge in Allah from the harm of those who might envy you by reciting *Surah Falaq* (113:5).
- **Adopt an attitude of gratitude.** In *Surah Ibrahim* (14:7) we learn that if you show gratitude, Allah will give you more to be grateful about, so being grateful not only protects you from the harm of those who might envy you but also increases your blessings.
- **Always be aware.** Remember that no fortune or misfortune can touch your life without the will of God, so be constantly aware of this fact. To go out there and be awesome, you also need to practice self-awareness.

In terms of being jealous of others, obviously some people are just straight up irritating, but if you find yourself hating on someone when they've said or done something, use this space to ask yourself what is it in them that you're jealous of.

Although falling into the comparison trap is something you'll have to fight against your whole life, don't lose sleep and time over what other people are doing. Lose sleep over what *you* are not doing.

Who am I jealous of?

How can I ask them for help?

Things to do when I feel envious of others:

Things to do when I think others are envious of me:

Meet Poetic Pilgrimage

Passionate Poets

Poetic Pilgrimage are a British Jamaican duo who are the first Muslim hip hop artists in Britain.

Did you know...

→ Muneera Rashida and Sukina Abdul Noor met in high school and discovered a shared love of music when they joined the school choir together.

→ They embraced Islam after learning about Malcolm X and have been spreading the message of Islam through their spoken word performances.

→ Poetic Pilgrimage have performed all over the world and explore topics of gender, faith, citizenship, and their Jamaican heritage through their performances.

"Unicorns have nothing on us."

CHAPTER EIGHTEEN

Tie Your Camel

By now you may be feeling like an impatient child sitting on the back-seat of the greatest journey of your life thinking *Are we nearly there yet?* The good news is that we almost are.

In this final chapter we're going to take inspiration from camels. Don't worry, I won't be telling you to go without food and water for days! Instead, we will be talking about taking responsibility and what happens when we blame every one else but ourselves when we don't achieve our goals.

This is the last part of our journey and it may feel a bit scary to go out there and put everything you've learned into action, but I promise to hold your hand as you try to figure out

What proverbial camels of yours must you tie for your dreams to come true?

I'm guessing that you probably don't own a camel or come across many where you live, but here in the Middle East, where I'm often stuck behind a truck full of livestock gawking at me in traffic, the camel *hadith* reminds me that I am the only person in this world who is solely responsible for achieving my crazy dreams.

Here's a quick history lesson for you. When Our Messenger saw a desert dweller leaving his camel untied one day, he questioned him about his carefree attitude. The Bedouin replied that there was no need to tie his camel because he had placed his trust in Allah to look after it. It sounds like a pretty honourable thing to do, but to this, our Messenger replied "Trust in Allah BUT tie your camel".

This famous *hadith* teaches me that if I really want to dream, du'a, and do, it's not about me relying on just the knowledge of my religion to help me succeed, or sitting on my bum, eating dinner by the TV, and just waiting for good things to happen. It's about me relying on myself to use that knowledge to own my success. It means that I tie my camel and have *tawaakul*! That I take the necessary action, and if it is beyond me, I find someone to help me.

Let's break down what trusting in Allah but tying your camel could mean for you.

1. Trusting Allah—having *tawaakul*

The first step to making your wildest dreams reality is believing in the ability of Allah to make you successful. Trusting Allah is trusting in something bigger than you to give you the strength you need to see your goal through.

Quick reminder: In Arabic, the word used to describe the act of trusting Allah is *tawaakul*. I used to sit back and wait for my dreams to come true, but then I realised that having *tawaakul* is about doing your utmost best to do what Allah has designed you to do, and then leaving the outcome to the will of God.

It's about assessing the things you have control over, trusting your-self to take the necessary action, and trusting Allah to do the rest.

It's about keeping your eyes on the sky but your feet on the ground, praying on one hand but being productive on the other. It's about setting your intentions and moving forward in faith, not sitting idly on your phone thinking positive thoughts.

It's about trusting the process.

2. Tying your camel—taking action

The second step to making your wildest dreams reality is taking action. A dream marked with a date becomes an ambition. An ambition broken down into stages becomes a strategy. A strategy backed up by action and *tawaakul* becomes a dream come true.

By now you'll have a very clear idea about your ambition, and you're learning to truly believe that if you are meant to fulfil your calling, it will never miss you. So trust your instinct and know that when Allah decides it's time for you to share your gift with the world, you will be unstoppable. Not unstoppable in the sense that everything will be easy as pie and you'll never be disappointed, defeated, or heartbroken again, but unstoppable in the sense that nothing and no-one can stop you moving closer to your goal.

Every action you take is shaped by your belief. If you believe your dream is impossible, your actions and behaviour will inevitably mirror that, but if you have *tawaakul* and believe to the core of your bones that God is behind you, that will shape your destiny.

To achieve your ambitions you need to be active, not passive. Being active means scheduling a time and place to work on your dream, because if something isn't scheduled, you're just leaving it to chance. Scheduling also allows you to make a contingency plan if things don't work out the way you wanted. For instance, if you fail to work out in the morning, you could make a backup plan to work out in the evening or the next day.

Another example of taking action (or tying your camel) is by seeking knowledge. In *Surah Al Alaq* (96:1), we learn about the first time Prophet Muhammad was given a revelation by Archangel Gibraeel who said "Read in the name of your Lord".

I love that the first call of action ever communicated to us was to *iqra*, to read. Not worship, not wake up, or any other verb. That this was the very first word Allah shared with us shows the status of reading, learning, or growing through knowledge, in Islam.

In Islam we are taught that although knowledge is power, knowledge without action is pretty much a waste of time. Taking action is being committed to lifelong learning. In an era of instant information, ignorance isn't bliss; it's a choice you get to make every day. When Allah tells us to seek knowledge, it doesn't necessarily mean going to university, it means pursuing knowledge throughout our life. In a world where we have access to information in the palm of our hands, it means we focus on educating ourselves instead of entertaining ourselves.

So, if there's one action that could take you much further than I ever could with my book, that action is to establish your relationship with the Quran, the mother of all self-improvement books.

My love and appreciation for the Quran only started in recent years when I began teaching my kids. I started memorising the short *surahs* along with them. Then I came across Nouman Ali Khan's lectures on YouTube and started studying the *tafsir*. I began trying to put what I learned into practice and started making small changes in my life. I became obsessed with learning more about the gems I found in each *surah*. I finally concluded that the Quran is very cool!

The Quran is full of tips and techniques and has the answers to every possible situation you may encounter when trying to live a life that you love. All you have to do is take the first step: *read*.

The truth is that you and you alone are responsible for who you become, because you are the only one in control of your life. Not your parents, not your friends, not your cousins, not your husband, not your mother-in-law, and no, not even your boss. You!!

I want you to dream big because dreams that are big fuel you, motivate you, and inspire you to take action. I want you to be brave and go after the things you want and never look back. I want you to know that everything is here to teach us a lesson. Every trial, every person we encounter, and every challenge we endure are all perfect preparation to make you into who you need to be.

Let me remind you of the (slightly rearranged) words of a great philosopher named Spiderman: With great responsibility comes great power.

I don't have an older sister, but I'd like to imagine that if I did, she'd be the kind of sister who would help me contour my face as she gave me a pep talk about taking ownership when shooting for the stars.

> **I want you to realise that there's a Muslimah inside you who you haven't met yet, and it's your responsibility to take the necessary action to discover her.**

I also like to imagine that she'd be the type to smack me lovingly on my forehead every time I felt sorry for myself and be the first to tell me that it's not okay to go through life blaming my insecurities, my anxieties, my fears, my failures, or even my burnt toast on something or someone other than myself.

Of course, I'm talking about a specific kind of self-pity here, because taking responsibility is not the same as taking the blame. Obviously, there are lots of things that can happen to us that are not in our control. We don't choose the body, family, or even era we're born into, and we certainly don't choose for bad things to happen to us.

Even though you're not always in control of what life throws at you, you are always in control of how you react. But blaming your circumstances, job, family, or childhood just so you can justify not becoming the best version of yourself, that is my idea of a pity party.

For many of us, blaming others is our favourite pastime. If we're really honest, it's our guilty pleasure. We luxuriate in the blame game because it's another addition to our collection of comfort blankets. Another wonderful place for us to bury our head and hide.

For years, I partied in pity. Sometimes I wallowed in it and other times I drowned in it. I have flirted with depression long enough to realise that it made me feel better temporarily when I didn't take ownership of my sad situations. But along the way, I also realised that the longer I stayed in my pity pit, the longer I stayed trapped in a victim mindset where nothing could change.

When we chug on by on the blame train, what we're doing is avoiding taking ownership for our own actions. We blame anything else because it's just so easy. But I want you to know that it's a terrible idea to keep falling back on something that happened last week, last month, last year, or even last decade. After a while, it just gets boring. Well, at least for me it did.

Whatever your situation, stop allowing your past to dictate your future. If you were on the receiving end of bad parenting, take the responsibility to parent yourself. If you studied at a school where the teacher took naps instead of teaching you, take the responsibility to teach yourself. If you were in a loveless marriage, take the responsibility to love yourself.

But whatever you do, don't use it as an excuse for who you are today. In *Surah Al A'raf* (7:23), we learn about a profound du'a made by Prophet Adam, which became the first du'a known to mankind. He said

**"Rabbana thalamna anfusana wa illam thakfirlanan watarhamna lanakuna minal khasirreen".
(Our Lord! We have sinned against ourselves and unless You grant us forgiveness and bestow Your mercy upon us, we shall most certainly be lost).**

Prophet Adam could have pointed the finger at the devil for enticing him to disobey God, but instead he chose to point the finger right back at himself. He acknowledged his mistakes and begged for forgiveness. And so one of the very first lessons taught to human beings was to take responsibility.

Look, I totally empathise that you've had to deal with some downright awful people or things. I feel your pain because I've been there too, but you know what else is awful? Awful is knowing that there are eight gates to Paradise and you didn't have what it takes to walk through a single one of them.

In *Surah Ash-Sharh* (94:6) Allah says "Indeed with hardship comes ease". We often confuse that verse by thinking *after* hardship follows ease, but that's not what Allah is saying here. It means that for every situation we face, no matter how difficult the challenge, there are also blessings in disguise, we also face ease. *Through* hardship comes ease.

Hard things don't necessarily happen *to* us, they happen *for* us.

I wanted to share this verse with you because I know that some of you may have dealt with or be dealing with some hard things and it may seem impossible to see past the trauma. You may feel your plans and passion will have to sit on the backburner for a while or maybe even forever.

Sis, I want you to know that even if you find yourself going through something so deep, so heart-breaking, so raw, don't let it deter you from chasing your aspirations because even your hardships serve a purpose.

Find the courage to look beyond the pain and search for the lesson it's trying to teach you. Don't miss the message because you are so consumed with hurt, shame, and blame. Take the responsibility to see past it and don't let it distract you from your dreams.

Those bullies from high school, they don't pay your electricity bills so they don't get to decide who you can or can't be. The marketers and the media may have a lot of information on you, but even they can't use that information to control you if you don't let them. And as for your parents, they don't need to feed and fend for you anymore, so the only person who should decide your future is you.

In *Surah Ar R'ad* (13:11), we learn that "Allah does not change the condition of a people unless they change themselves". This means that if you're not willing to take the necessary action to change your unhappy situation, then whether you like it or not, you don't get to be happy. Remember, your brain's job is to keep you safe, not happy. It's your job to keep you happy.

You get one chance to live this life, so stop accepting less than you deserve. Stop letting your dreams drift by and missing out on your greatest chance to butterfly.

Your Turn!

In this final section, I would like you think about all the actions you need to take to make your dream come true. What proverbial camels of yours must you tie?

What were you designed to do?

You have one chance with this gift called life. What are you going to do with it?

Step 1: Dream

Write down your 1 big dream

Step 2: Du'a

Write down 2 du'as (connect *dunya* with *akhirah*)

Step 3: Do

Write down 3 things you need to do to achieve your dream

Now go!

Start living a life that you love!
All you have to do is Dream, Du'a, and Do

Meet Malala Yousafzai

An Amazing Activist

Malala is a Pakistani advocate for education, especially for young girls.

Did you know...

- At seventeen years old, Malala became the youngest person in the world to win the Nobel Peace Prize.
- Malala was shot for speaking out on behalf of young girls and their right to an education.
- She has written several books about her experiences and has spoken publicly all over the world, including at the United Nations.

"One child, one teacher,
one book, one pen
can change the world."

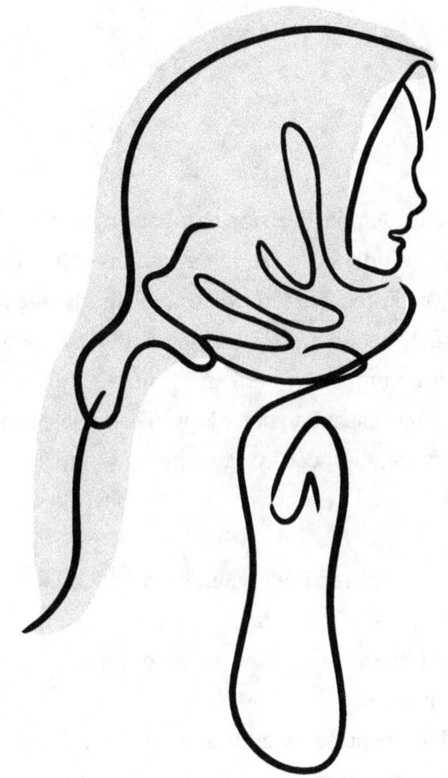

Afterword

A decade back, I made the decision to follow my wildest dream to set up home in the Middle East. I didn't even know that this small city where I now live existed, but I knew I wanted more from the life I was living at the time. Looking back, I understand why everyone around me thought I was completely bonkers for quitting my perfectly good job, convincing my husband to quit his even better job, and putting our apartment up for rent, especially when my new employment contract and plane tickets didn't even arrive until two weeks before we were to leave!

I remember how scared I felt when we made the wild decision to pack up and start again from scratch. I didn't know if it would all work out or not, but I knew this: I knew I had to close my eyes and go for it. Come what may.

Fast forward to the present day and luckily for me, my cowboy plan did work out. I have to say that packing my marriage, my kids, and a lifetime of clothes into a series of leopard-print suitcases was by no means an easy task, nor was it as glamorous as those bloggers make it sound. It was a bumpy ride, especially for the first couple of years as we got used to our new surroundings, but *alhamdulillah,* every night as I tuck my kids into bed, I know that this epic move to the great unknown, daring to dream, was an adventure well worth taking.

As I sit here contemplating how I managed to achieve this life, which is so different to the one I knew, I know the answer is Dream, Du'a, Do. These three words have been etched into me for over a decade now; they are the first words I write in each new journal.

A few years ago, I began thinking a lot about why these words are so powerful to me, and why these words weren't around when I needed them the most, which led me to wondering why the book I needed hadn't yet been written. And so I opened up my laptop and began to write for myself—the things I knew, the things that had worked for me, the things I still needed to learn.

As the chapters of this book unfolded, so did my dream to get it into your hands. I had no idea how to get it published or what I needed to do to get it published. That seemed like such a wild dream. But the whole experience has reminded me of the beautiful verse in *Surah Baqarah* (2:286) where we are told that "Allah does not burden a soul beyond it can bear." Our soul would not be burdened with our dreams if we didn't have what it takes to see it through. Once again, I was taught that if you have the intention to do something good, the Almighty will make it easy for you. When I eventually found my publisher, I prayed *istikhara,* closed my eyes, and went for it, and the fact that you are reading my book is testament to the fact that everything I have talked about can be achieved.

I practiced what I preached in *Dream, Du'a, Do.* And here it is in your hands. Never ever underestimate the power of dreaming. Never underestimate the power of du'a, and most importantly, never underestimate your own power to do what it takes to achieve your goals.

This book is written for all the marvellous Muslimahs out there who are three steps away from breaking boundaries, shattering glass ceilings, and changing the world.

Aspire not to have more but to be more. The world needs more women like us. What the world doesn't need is another Muslimah who is frozen by the fear that she needs to be more pious, more qualified, more prepared, more experienced, more expert, more gorgeous than she already is before she can share her ideas and change the world.

The world needs the woman you were created to be.

You are ready.

Reading list

This is not just my reference list; this is your reading list!

Each of these books has had a profound impact on my life and the way I think. As you can see, I have it in three key sections that pertain to each of the specific topics: dream, du'a, or do. My advice is to take a quick look at each book—even if it means just reading a sample on your Kindle—and see if it speaks to you or not.

For sure, there will be some books you connect with straightaway and others that doesn't quite speak to you in the way that you would like, so go ahead and skip those; it's perfectly okay! You may also find it useful to scribble down your inspirations from these books on the note pages here; they can help you with the Your Turn sections too.

Dream

→ *Awaken the Giant Within,* by Tony Robbins
→ *Rewire Your Brain,* by John B. Arden
→ *The Secret,* by Rhonda Byrn

- → *Big Magic,* by Elizabeth Gilbert
- → *Find Your Why,* by Simon Sineck
- → *Limitless,* by Jim Kwik
- → *The Art of Being Brilliant,* by Andy Cope
- → *The Magic of Thinking Big,* by David J Schwartz

Du'a

- → The Holy Quran, by Allah (obviously)
- → *In the Early Hours: Reflections on Spiritual and Self-Development,* by Khurram Murad
- → *Du'a: The Weapon of the Believer,* by Yasir Qadhi
- → *The Three Abandoned Prayers,* by Shaykh Adnaan Aali Uroor
- → *Revive Your Heart,* by Nouman Ali Khan

Do

- → *Mindset,* by Carol Dweck
- → *Grit,* by Angela Duckworth
- → *Daring Greatly,* by Brene Brown
- → *The 5 AM Club,* by Robin Sharma
- → *The Productive Muslim,* by Mohammad Faris
- → *Thanks!,* by Robert A. Emmons

Useful Websites

→ Quran.com

→ Sunnah.com

→ Sujood.com

Useful apps

→ Happyfeed

→ MuslimPal

→ Athaan

→ Pinterest

Glossary of Terms

A

Adhaan: call to prayer

Adhkars: remembrance of God

Alhamdulillah: All praise and gratitude belongs to God

AllahhuAkbar: God is the Greatest

Amanah: fulfilling or upholding a trust

Ashurah: the first month of the Muslim calendar

Ayah/ayahs: verses from the Quran

B

Barakah: blessings

D

Deen: religion

Dhikr: remembrance of God

Du'a: prayer, supplication

Du'a al ibadah: prayer of worshipping

Du'a al mas'alah: prayer to ask for something

Dunya: world

F

Fard: something that is obligatory

Fiqh: the theory of Islamic law

Fitra: a state of purity

H

Hadith/ahadith: sacred saying from Prophet Muhammad

Hajj: the greater Muslim pilgrimage

Halaqah: study circle

Hasad: envy

Hijab: headscarf

Hijabi: a Muslim woman who wears a headscarf

Hisnul Muslim: fortress of the Muslim

I

Insan: human beings

Isti'aathah: seeking refuge from the outcast devil

Istighfar/astaghfirullah: asking for forgiveness

Istikhara: asking for guidance

J

Jinn/jinns: supernatural spirits

Jumu'ah: Friday prayers

K

Kaaba: place of worship in Mecca

Kashi'een: someone who can pray with full sincerity and concentration

Khushoo: to pray with heightened awareness of God; to pray with sincerity and full attention

Kifara: the return of God what you give out to the world

L

Laylatul qadr: the night of power

M

Masjid: mosque

Muslimah: a female Muslim

N

Noor: light

Q

Qadr: fate

Qibla: the direction of the *kaaba*

R

Rabi ul awal: the third month in the Islamic calendar

Rajjab: seventh month in the Islamic Calendar

Rizq: sustenance

S

Sabr: patience

Sadaqah Jariyah: the act of voluntarily making a long-term charitable contribution that continues to benefit someone other than yourself

Sa'i: to strive or to pursue something

Salaam: peace

Salah: obligatory prayers

Shabban: The eighth month of the Islamic Calendar

Shahadah: testimony of faith

Shaytaan: devil

Sujood: prostration in prayer

Sunnah: ways of the prophet

T

Tafsir: explanation of the Quran

Tahajjud: a special act of worship conducted in the last third of the night

Takbeer: God is the Greatest

Tasbih: prayer beads used to glorify God

Tashahud: a position of prayer

Tawaakul: having trust in God

Tazkiyah: self-improvement

U

Ummah: the Muslim community

Umrah: minor pilgrimage

W

Wasawaas: whispers

Wudhoo: ritual washing usually done in preparation before praying

Y

Yakeen: to have sincere faith

Z

Zakat: charity

Zam zam: holy water

About
the author

Ruzina is living her best life in Abu Dhabi with her husband and two children. They drive her mad but she can't imagine a single day of her life without them! Apart from being a writer she also has a master's degree in Leadership and Management in Education and has been working as a teacher/teacher trainer for adult learning institutes in the UK as well as UAE for too many years.

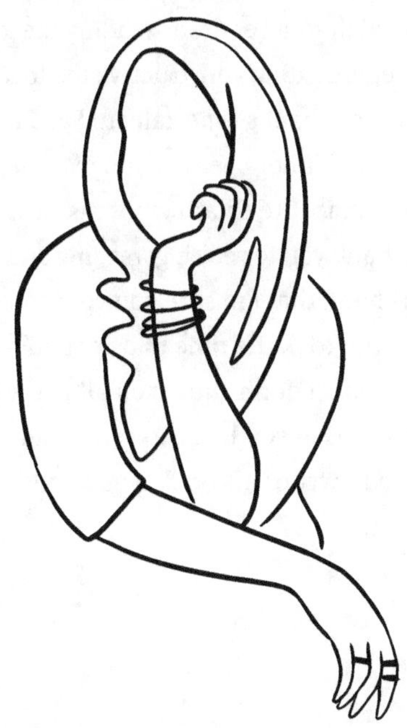

Gratitude

First and foremost, *alhamdulillah*. All thanks and praise belongs to the Almighty, the One who blessed me with the ability to share my message with the world. To You we belong, and to You we return. Please forgive me for any mistakes or shortcomings I have made in this book and please make it a means of *sadaqa jariyah* for me.

I am immensely grateful to my army of friends, colleagues, and family members who gave in to my pestering at all hours of the day and tirelessly read draft after draft, sending me love wherever in the world they were, providing constructive feedback and encouraging me to keep writing. Thanks especially to Syla, my book would have never been born had it not been for you planting the seeds of inspiration in the first place. To Rifath who was the first person I shared my work with: thank you for editing, reading and re-reading so many versions of this book that I'm sure you've memorised it all by now! And to Zaynab who took the time to print and read my first draft as if it were a real book. I don't think you all know how valuable your support was to me. Had you laughed your heads off when I told you about my dream to write this book, you would not be holding it in your hands today.

A special thanks to my best friend and husband, Sami, who couldn't give a monkey's about this book but who nonetheless made sure our kids were well nourished, well groomed, and well out of my way while I spent almost the last two years obsessed with this project. A special thanks to my brother and sister and parents who also couldn't give a toss about my latest venture but at least promised to keep a copy of it on their bookshelf! You are my rocks and you keep me grounded, thank you.

To all the literature I have read to date: Your words have shaped me in ways you can never imagine. I am who I am because of you, so from the bottom of my heart, thank you. To the greatest writer of all, my legendary grandmother: Your story will forever inspire me. As I now near the age of forty, I realise just how young you were when you became a widow, and as I live thousands of miles away from home I now understand just how lonely you must have felt without your family nearby. But despite your heartbreak, you poured your pain onto pages. Those pages were then published and you became a celebrated writer in Bangladesh. Thank you for inspiring me.

To all the resources I have used, particularly sunnah.com, quran.com, and sujood.com: Your work is invaluable to the Muslim *ummah*. To all the amazing Muslimahs I have mentioned in this book, and to Faris Al Hammadi: thank you for checking the authenticity of my work.

Last but not least, can I get a standing ovation for the team that made this all happen: The Dreamwork Collective! Kira, it is an absolute honour to be a part of this fabulous powerhouse that you have built. I don't know how you do it, but you make it all look so effortless. Special thanks to Thalia who has not only been my editor but also my mentor through this entire process. Your editorial support was above and beyond the call of duty and I will never forget your kindness! I also want to thank Heike for my wonderful cover design as well as Kasia for the amazing illustrations and typesetting; this project would not have been possible without you all!

Thank you for joining me on this journey.

Big hugs xx

Extra Notes